Alan Perry was born in Swansea a
of Art. His first collection of poem:
Award and was published in 196
Wires (1970), *Fires on the Common*
Edge Press published several of hi
er Stories (1977) and *Castaway Pre*
ries in the following year. His verse play *Occupied Territories* (co-written with Lloyd Rees) was premiered at the UK Year of Literature in 1995 and the book of the play, *To Liu and All Mankind* was published in the same year. *Music You Don't Normally Hear* (1998) used field research and edited transcripts of interviews with homeless people. He later adapted the book for the stage and it has had many performances since then, the last under the direction of film-maker Karl Francis. An artist as well as a poet, he abandoned poetry in the eighties to concentrate on the short story and to develop his painting. He exhibits his work widely in galleries, on the net and on his own website: *alanperry.1hwy.com*. In 1993, the Glynn Vivian Art Gallery published *Shards*, a collection of paintings and poems and in 1998, he illustrated *LMNTRE Poems* by Vernon Watkins. Last year, Moonstone Press published *Dreaming from North to South*, his New and Selected Poems. Alan Perry now paints and writes in Swansea with his wife Jean, who is also an artist.

by the same author:

Poetry:

Characters
Live Wires
Fires on the Common
Winter Bathing
Shards (paintings and poems)
Dreaming from North to South (*New and Selected Poems, 2006*)

Prose:

Road Up and Other Stories
55999 and Other Stories
U Turns (the early 'Perkins' stories)
To Liu and All Mankind (poems and stories)
Music You Don't Normally Hear (the Documentary)

Drama:

Occupied Territories (with Lloyd Rees)
Music You Don't Normally Hear (the Performance)

DAYS OF THE COMET

New and Selected Stories

Alan Perry

> To Ju-Pu
> any friend of Gill's
> is a friend of mine.
> All the best, Alan

MOONSTONE PRESS
2007

First published in Great Britain, 2007

© Alan Perry

Published by Moonstone Press
3 Raleigh Close
Sketty
Swansea
SA2 8LE
e-mail: moonstone.press@ntlworld.com

All rights reserved. No part of this publication may be reproduced, stored in a retrieval system or transmitted in any form or by any means, electronic, mechanical, photocopying, recording or otherwise, without the prior permission of the author.

ISBN 0-9552640-1-4
      978-0-9552640-1-6

Printed by Gomer Press, Llandysul, Wales

Cover and inner design by Gareth Perry
Cover painting by Alan Perry: 'Interloper 1'

This book is presented as a work of fiction
and is dedicated to Gareth, David and Cécille

and also to Arthur Smith (1927-2006)

Acknowledgements:

Some of these stories first appeared, in earlier versions, in the booklet *55999 and Other Stories* (Castaway Press, 1978). Others have appeared, also in earlier versions, in the anthology *Dismays and Rainbows* (Gomer Press, 1979), the two-man anthology *To Liu and All Mankind* (Tooth and Nail Press, 1995), and the following magazines: *Planet, New Welsh Review, Cambrensis, Swagmag and Writer's Muse.*

May 13th. won first prize in the Swansea Advertiser Dylan Thomas short story writing competition.

Contents

12 Felix Close	9
The Atelier Perkins	15
Mr. Mallin	19
Acute	27
The Bird: A Story	33
Time Piece	39
Fixture	43
The Blue Bird of Happiness on a Plate	47
To Liu and All Mankind	77
After the Deluge	79
Storm in a Teacup	83
May 13th	85
Starters	91
Power	97
Days of the Comet	99
Rhyme, Wine and Worse	105
Personal Best	117
Snow	119
Night on a Bare Mountain	123
Upside Down Roses	129
Mort Dies	135
Dowsers	141
The Mattress	147
Monkey Business	149
The Great Onanist	151
Culture	157
Friends, Romans, Countrymen	163
The Tunisian Open '97	175
Second Coming	179
Beauty and the Beast	187
Medicine	197
Medical	203
Apocalypse Then	211

12 Felix Close

You needed a car to get there. Or else you caught a train and then a bus which dropped you a mile away on the dual carriageway and you walked the rest. There was a printed map on the back of the appointments card to help you, but it was dark when Perkins got there and doubly difficult to find.

He hadn't been to the surgery in Dr McVey's house before. It was on a new, mock-Scandinavian estate way out in the Greenback Belt. He walked past the place at first because he was too early. A glossy car stood in the drive and a light shone above the front door. Where the pavement ended there was suddenly open countryside and only wire fencing stretching away into the darkness. He stood by the fence for a moment looking out over the fields towards the distant lights of the town. Minute headlamps flickered, sending pale shafts of light criss-crossing upwards into the night…

Mrs McVey answered the door. She smiled and led him into a smart front room and took his coat. The Doctor wouldn't be long: would he take a seat, please. Perkins sank into a plush leather armchair and felt as though he was sitting in the display window of Eddershaw's. Everything was immaculate: Art Nouveau lamp stand, thick-pile Wilton, some superbly gilt-framed but awful reproduction prints, a stand full of fancy walking-sticks and a ceramic tiled coffee table with half a dozen National Geographicals and Country Lifes.

There was someone already in the Consulting Room. He couldn't quite make out who it was or what they were saying. It sounded like a woman: the voice confidential and measured – a steady, continual monotone. He picked up a magazine and read half a page about Buddhists in Ceylon and a paragraph about leaf-eating ants in the Amazon. Then he went through his pockets one by one, studying documents and scraps of paper with the ancient germs of poems on. The muffled monotone droned on. He twisted and turned and was about to break wind when a car pulled up in the drive outside. He waited, but nobody came.

He was studying a map of the London Underground in an old diary when the electronic voice suddenly crackled into life: *'I keep telling myself it must be me! I keep on asking myself why? Why? What's wrong with me...I've tried and tried God knows I've tried...if only he'd* **say** *something, but he just sits there...'*

Perkins edged his chair closer to the door. The voice went on and on:

'it's this terrible silence...if only he'd lose his temper and hit me or throw something. But he just sits there like a ventriloquist's dummy. It's as though he's got no feelings at all...'

This seemed almost worth coming for. He leaned across, straining to hear. How much longer could she keep it up? McVey must have switched off ages ago. On his glasses were painted two large, alert and sympathetic eyes. A Dictaphone concealed under his blotting paper played a continual *'Yes'* and *'Mmm'* and *'Yes –uh-huh – I see.'*

'...he knew how much that dog meant to me. I've always wanted an Afghan Hound. And then the other day I came home and he'd sold it – bought me a wire-haired terrier instead...'

Perhaps McVey wasn't in there at all. She was consulting a life-sized cardboard cut-out. The real flesh-and-blood McVey was in the living room watching Star Trek or playing Ludo with the kids.

The door bell chimed and Perkins adjusted his chair as Mrs McVey answered it. Into the room stepped a middle-aged couple: the man, short and bald and moon-faced; the woman, tall and thin and sharp-featured. Mrs McVey hung up their coats and they sat down opposite Perkins. The woman snatched up a magazine and began reading it, quickly.

'Nasty weather,' said the man. 'Good job we brought our coats – there's a touch of frost about – '

'...I keep on getting these obscene phone calls. I know its him – but he keeps on trying to disguise his voice. And then he starts this heavy-breathing business, and when I say I know it's him – he hangs up. He's trying to drive me mad...'

The newcomer glanced at his watch and smiled: 'Been waiting long?' he said.

'About twenty minutes,' Perkins said. 'There's some woman in there now. Very mixed up. Husband won't speak to her.'

'Strong, silent type, eh?' said the man.

'Sounds like. He sold her Afghan Hound and bought her a wire-haired terrier instead.'

'There's some funny people about.'

The Consulting Room door opened. A well-dressed woman in her fifties came out, dabbing at her eyes with a handkerchief. McVey followed close behind. He was shorter than the woman, pale-faced and concerned behind thick-lensed glasses. He helped her on with her coat and saw her to the door: '– three of these of these four times a day, Mrs Lloyd-Thomas,' he said, pressing a small phial into her hands. She stepped out into the night and McVey followed a few paces behind, calling after her reassuringly. He came back in shuddering from the cold and, with a friendly sweep of the arm, motioned Perkins into the Consulting Room.

McVey seemed to have shrunk since last time. He pulled out a folder from the bottom drawer of his desk and flicked through the pages for a full minute, then he looked over the top of his glasses, smiled and said, 'How're you feeling?'

'Better than I was,' Perkins said. 'My mouth feels very dry. I've got blurred vision. I'm slightly constipated and I seem to talk a heck of a lot.'

'Normal side-effects,' said McVey. 'Eating?' He simulated the action with a hand.

'I'm on a diet of tuna fish, Ryvita and unsweetened grapefruit juice. Lost two stone in a month.'

'Don't overdo it,' McVey said. 'Any more panic bouts?'

'Only two. The first in Tesco's shopping with the wife. I broke out in a cold sweat and had to run home. The second time was in School. I was on Yard Duty when I had the shivers. I had to go and sit in the Staff Room.'

McVey nodded. There was a pause as he turned a page and slowly turned it back again. There were always a lot of pauses with McVey.

'Morbid fears?'

'Nearly all gone, Doctor.'

'Nightmares? Feelings of unreality?'

'Much fewer and farther between. I've even started writing again – '

Another, even longer, pause: 'And what about sex? Sometimes we find these pills suppress the sexual drive and we have to put people on something else.'

'Never been better. What would you say I was, Doctor: a manic depressive?'

'I wouldn't go as far as to say that – not exactly. Your condition is endogenous. You were born with it. We don't know why some people are or what causes it exactly, but we think it's some sort of chemical deficiency in the brain. It seems to occur in cycles – usually every three years or so. It's rather like a wave: at the moment you're just rising out of a trough. In a few years you'll probably sink back into another trough – and so on and so on, probably for the rest of your life. But not to worry, Mr Perkins. We know we can control it. We may not know how or why we can, but the important thing is that the medication really works. Can you remember the state you were in when you first came to see me? And now look at you: almost your old self again and perfectly able to cope.' He closed the folder and smiled: 'How's the job going?'

'Fine – I quite enjoy it now.'

'Good. But don't forget what I told you. Don't mention to your employers that you've been coming to see me. They may not be quite so understanding – and they could make things awkward for you.'

McVey got up, reached in a drawer and pulled out a cardboard box. He wouldn't want to see Perkins again unless there was a recurrence. He rummaged among an assortment of multi-coloured phials and dug out two small plastic tubes containing the familiar pink and green capsules. He pressed the tubes into Perkins' hand like a kind old uncle distributing Smarties: 'Four of these three times a day,' he said.

Back at the railway station, Perkins had an hour to kill. The Buffet was closed. He stared through the window at the counter: tantalizing rows of sandwiches, plastic oranges floating on an ice-cold sea of Quosh. There was no-one in sight. Next to the darkened Gents was a cage on wheels full of bundles of newspapers and magazines. Perkins glanced around, unzipped and had a pee standing behind them, trying to make out the headlines as the hot stream steamed at his feet. He walked slowly to the very end of the platform and then back. There were no benches – not even a vending machine. He wandered up and down hands dug in pockets trying to keep warm. He peered into the red bucket full of sand. He stood in the middle of the pitch-black Waiting Room and closed his eyes and clenched his fists and waited…

It was ten o' clock when he caught the Nine-thirty. He stepped off the cold stone platform into the bedlam of the Buffet: Dante's Inferno on wheels: everyone singing and shouting, the floor awash with beer and rolling with cans and straws and plastic cups. The Irish were going home for Christmas.

Perkins bought two cans and sat down opposite a ruddy-faced man dressed like a farmer. At the adjacent table, two youths and an elder man – a big greasy individual – were hunched up together, a rout of cans In front of them. The youths were laughing and cursing – performing for the two girls who sat opposite. One was a pretty brunette flaked out against the window, the other a frizzy blonde, heavily mascara-ed and only half asleep.

The night shrieked by in a void. Mascara started to sing, softly at first, the Number One hit. She sang it with great emotion – not in the style or tempo of Rock, but as though it were an ancient Irish ballad. Her voice seemed to gather strength as she realized she was being listened to but then, at a most poignant moment, she cursed out loud and shut up. Everyone cheered and shouted for more, but she'd had enough of singing. The two youths staggered to the Bar, leaving the greasy man still sitting. Mascara studied him through half-closed eyes for a moment, then she said: 'What're yer sittin der all on yer own for? Come an sit here. I hate to see a fella sittin all on his own.'

She shifted up against her friend and the man moved in next to her. The farmer turned to Perkins, who couldn't take his eyes off Mascara and the big greasy bloke. He'd been up to Bristol he said, to sell a car. 'There's a lovely town, Bristol!' He'd driven the car up in the morning, sold it at a profit, and now he was coming back. He'd had a grand time. Oh yes – he'd had a lovely day...

Greasy was whispering something to Mascara...

' – *What d'yer tink I am!*' she snapped. '*What sort of a girl d'yer take me for? Get away wit yer! G'wan – get away!*'

The man moved away, a sheepish grin on his face and the girl tossed back her fuzzy blonde head and closed her eyes.

There were no lights on when Perkins got home. He tiptoed upstairs and undressed in the dark on the landing. Through the window he could see the Town spread out below; the sea pinpricked with lights. In notebooks downstairs he had a score of phrases for the way moonlight glazed the rooftops round the Bay.

He felt for the edge of the bed and drew back the sheet. The springs creaked as he eased himself in and the dark hump of his wife stirred.

'It's alright, love,' he said. 'I missed the last bus – '

'Get your cold feet off my back – ' she groaned and shifted over.

Perkins warmed his hands between his legs and lay still. Later, when the blood had begun to flow, he stroked her back under the thin nylon and looked out at the silvery blue through the gap he had left in the curtains. He imagined the ferry boat, an hour out: decks deserted, the girls asleep in the still Saloon: Mascara with her head on Greasy's shoulder, silently gliding home...

The Atelier Perkins

The shed was due for delivery that morning. During a lull in a lesson, Perkins drew a little plan of the interior to remind himself of where everything was going to go: filing cabinet in one corner, bookcase in another, desk by window, fire near door…He labelled everything, even drawing a circle on the square of the chair to represent a bird's eye view of his head and compiling a check-list of his needs: wallpaper, putty, padlock, anti-theft device…

At the end of the day he drove home at some speed, put the car away quickly, skipped up the steps…and there it was at the bottom of the garden: standing alone and strangely alien – a Time Machine dropped in from outer space: six by four and a bright orange colour with a green felt roof. The whole garden smelt of the cedarwood finish. He unfastened the black metal door clasp. It was pristine and bare inside with dark-orange walls. The floor was crisscrossed with the lorry driver's boot-prints and creaked when he set foot on it. He closed the door behind him and stood there in the duskiness looking out through the three small panes of glass. A segment of sea, windswept and grey, was framed by the branches of the bay tree. He crouched down to get the view he would have from his writing desk …

When he went indoors his wife was standing at the sink peeling potatoes. He was just about to grab her from behind and plant a huge kiss on her neck when Mathew burst in to ask if he could go in the shed. 'No!' she snapped, still without turning. 'That's Daddy's private little sanctuary. None of us must go anywhere near there.'

Perkins decided to forego the kiss and give tea a miss. 'Got to post some letters,' he said and went back out.

It was dark by the time he returned. There was a circular piece of card pinned to the shed door now with CHEZ MOI crudely felt-tipped on it. He unpinned the card and went in. It was cold and dark inside with only a faint light from the windows. Through the glass he could see the black silhouettes of the bay tree and the amber and white necklaces of light bordering the sea. He stayed quite a while before going indoors, pleased that he could see the lightship's light and the lighthouse in either the standing or the crouched position.

The next day, Saturday, Perkins drove the family into Town. As well as the shopping, he managed to buy several of the items on his list and secrete them, without too much fuss, in the car. In the afternoon, while the others were watching TV, he went down to examine the shed more closely. He noticed the floor was sagging in several places – so much so that from the inside he could see daylight through the cracks. He gathered together a pile of slates and old off-cuts of wood he kept stored in the coal shed and set about propping up the floor. It wasn't easy. When he'd levered up one side and inserted the pieces under the wooden cross ties, he found the opposite end was sagging even more. As time wore on, he graduated from slates and bits of wood to whole bricks so that eventually he could see clearly underneath from one end to the other. The floor now seemed to be sagging in the centre, so he got several old planks and a couple of broom sticks and poked and wedged them underneath. As darkness began to fall he was bathed in sweat, even though the day had been a chilly one, and his back was covered in scratches where it had grazed against the bay tree. The floor still wasn't perfectly true but would have to do for the time being.

On the Sunday afternoon, his father called to do the wiring. He drilled a hole through the lounge window and one through a wall of the shed and ran a heavy duty cable between the two. After he'd gone, Perkins waited until it was completely dark before going down to the shed to switch on. The electric fire creaked slowly into life and he stood there looking out. With the light on, it wasn't so easy now to see the sea: the reflection of the interior of the shed and his own staring face were in the way.

On the Monday, he began cutting lino for the floor and stapling up some wallpaper. A lifelong arachnophobic, he particularly didn't want to leave any openings for spiders, so he went over the place with a fine tooth comb, blocking up every visible crack and cranny. Pretty soon the place was cluttered up with odd lengths and off-cuts of lino and wallpaper so that he could hardly move. It started to rain and in a while there was a tap on the door. He half-opened it, leaving just enough room to admit Owain. 'Mummy wants a cup of tea,' he said. 'You've gotto come and make it now or there'll be hell to play.'

Perkins held a strip of wallpaper up to the ceiling. 'Hold this here,' he said, 'and whatever you do, keep it straight – ' Owain got up on a chair and held it while Perkins stapled. It was much quicker work with two pairs of hands and after they'd hung the first strip they went on to a second and a third. Rain beat around them. In the middle of hanging the fourth run, just as Perkins was going to fire his second staple, the light went out. He cursed in the darkness and was about to let go of the wallpaper when the light came back on again. Two seconds later it went off and then on – off and on and finally off and stayed off. 'That's you mother playing silly buggers,' Perkins said. 'It'd be alright if I stapled the cable in the dark, wouldn't it!'

'Perfectly alright,' Owain said. 'If Mummy's switched off in the house that would mean the cable was dead – '

The papering took three days. During that time, whenever he was needed, the light would flick off and on repeatedly or, in an emergency, a brick would land suddenly and without warning, on the roof above his head. During a heavy downpour, he discovered the windows needed puttying. He did that and the same evening laid some old bedroom carpet – an eight by six foot section from under Mathew's bed – with the promise of a new carpet for him at an unspecified future date. When everything was finished, he brought down his desk and the papers and files and various reference books he'd need; his typewriter and finally a few inspirational pictures: one of Schubert, one of Blake another of Baudelaire another of him and his wife sitting on a stile during their courting days…

Then he sat down at the desk for the very first time in that place and picked up his pen in readiness to write his maiden poem. He was comfortably aware that mementos of loved-ones surrounded him: his grandfather's penknife – which he'd used to cut the wallpaper – his grandmother's small horseshoe-shaped mirror, his mother's electric fire…

He looked at himself, pen-poised, in the bay tree. Not a draught anywhere. Everything warm and snug. He got up, switched off a bar of the fire and sat down again. The top of the desk felt slightly clammy. A few drops of rain were still falling outside where the lightship and lighthouse flicked relentlessly in counterpoint: off and on, off and on, the lights of Ilfracombe still faintly visible through the darkness beyond. All at once, there was a small spider dangling on a thread in front of him, inches below the blazing lightbulb. He dropped his pen and sat frozen, staring at it for a moment: its horribly intricate body, curled-up legs twitching…Then slowly, very slowly, he reached across for the nearest book – M-Z of the Reader's Digest Great Encyclopaedic Dictionary – and, quick-as-a-flash, squashed it against the glass.

Mr. Mallin

The call came late one January night. It was from some bloke called Mallin who'd seen the write-up of Perkins' recent exhibition of paintings in the Evening Echo and wondered whether Perkins could help him out.

His voice sounded strained and there were long pauses between his words. He'd just been released from Sully Hospital – 'heart trouble' that's why he sounded so breathless – and had seen Perkins' photo in the paper and said to himself that *there* was a man who might be able to help him out. He didn't want to discuss matters over the phone but could Perkins see his way to going out there that evening because things had been so bad of late, he was seriously thinking of ending it all.

It took Perkins only a couple of minutes to get his car out. He ignored his wife's pleas for caution, told her he might be gone a while, then set out for the address Mallin had given him. It was a cold, frosty night. On the way he had visions of arriving too late, of dragging the old man from a gas-filled room or talking him down from a ninth storey ledge with police cars and fire engines and a whole swarm of sightseers gathered below. He was there in less than ten minutes.

Talfryn Court wasn't hard to find even by night. By day he'd passed it often enough on his way to School – an ugly, shit-coloured concrete monolith of stacked windows and balconies, towering over a dingy council estate. It was the kind of place where you could be mugged for a bag of crisps or be sitting dead in front of your TV set for weeks before anyone came and found you.

He parked under a lamppost, locked his car and hurried over the cracked flagstones to the front entrance. Only one light on the ground floor was working. He made towards the lift, feeling in his overcoat pocket for the wrench he'd brought along, just in case. The cubicle smelt of stale urine and vomit and he was glad to reach the ninth floor to be able to breathe again. There were six doors on this level and 9B was the second of them. Perkins rapped on the door and waited. After a moment, a chain rattled and a bolt slid back and the door opened – only a few inches at first, wide enough for an emaciated, ghastly pale face to peer through the gap.

'Mr Perkins,' both men said simultaneously.

The door opened fully. Standing in the shadows was a tall, scarecrow of a man, with grey hair and large, watery-blue eyes. He was dressed in shiny grey waistcoat, collarless off-white shirt buttoned at the top and grey trousers that stopped just short of his ankles. He greeted Perkins like a long-lost friend, pumping his hand vigorously, and led him from the cramped hallway into an even more cramped living room. It was cell-shaped, dim-lit and chill. A roughly made bed stood in one corner of the room and a small table crowded with medicine bottles stood in the other. The wallpaper was a washed-out dun with nails sticking out but no pictures. Next to the bed was an ancient armchair.

'Please take a seat, Mr Perkins,' Mallin said.

'No – *you* take the chair,' Perkins said. '*You're* the invalid.'

' – but I *insist*.'

Perkins sat in the armchair and Mallin perched awkwardly on the edge of the bed, his long, bony wrists draped over his knees. He apologized to Perkins over and over for dragging him out at that unearthly hour but he'd been absolutely at his wits end. He'd have offered him a cup of tea but the gas stove was on the blink, he said, offering him a cigarette instead. Perkins declined and Mallin lit up and coughed out a mouthful of smoke. Between gasps, he began to relate the convoluted history of his many ailments and misfortunes. It had all started when his wife and child died. He was only 25 and she was pregnant when they found out she had TB. Their deaths had knocked him for six. The shock had given rise to a duodenal ulcer which had burst eight times. They were going to put a tube in his chest but then the doctor decided against it: it was too near the main artery. As it was, he'd been out of hospital just three weeks. He'd worked all his life – up until the present trouble, that was – in a munitions factory in Bridgend during the War, then as a night watchman in the Oil Refinery. He'd led a good Christian life but couldn't get along to chapel as much as he used to. The welfare people had brought him a load of old clothes but he was so independent he didn't like asking people for help. He had no radio, no television, no close friends he could turn to and all his relatives were dead and gone. So if Perkins could just see his way to doing him one little favour, it would tide him over a rough period and make him eternally grateful…

Perkins' wife was watching the late film when he got back. She turned down the volume and switched on the table-lamp. 'How did it go?' she said.

    Perkins didn't want to say too much. 'Okay,' he said.
    'Just *okay?*'
    'Well, he was in a bit of a mess.'
    'What sort of a mess?'
    'Ill-health mostly – and financial difficulties.'
    '*Financial difficulties!* You didn't lend him any money, did you?'
    'Yes.'
    'How much?'
    'How much d'you think?'
    'A pound? A fiver…? How **much**!'
    'Twenty.'
    '**Twenty pounds!** Oh God, you bloody fool. He's *got* to be a con man. What did he say? How did he – '

Perkins told her to calm down: she hadn't heard the full story yet. She should have seen the conditions Mallin was living under! The place was an absolute hell-hole. No radio, no TV, no pictures on the walls. If either of them had to live there they'd have jumped straight off the balcony or put their head in the oven a long time ago…

The next day, in their dinner hour, Perkins and his wife drove out to Talfryn Court. They had with them a large cardboard box containing an assortment of groceries, three blankets and an old electric fire. When they knocked at 9B there was no answer. They tried a second and third time with the same result. Finally, they left the box with a teenage girl living in 9A, together with a scribbled note: *Dear Mr Mallin – Called but you were out. Please accept these few things from my wife and myself – with every good wish for the future, Alvin and Liz Perkins.*

On the way down they shared the lift with two women and Perkins' wife enquired about Mallin.

'What floor's e on, luv?'

'Ninth.'

'Whas e look like?'

'Tall, thin, elderly – '

'Oh, I knows im! Tall, thin, elderly – with a bit of a stoop. Number 9B.'

'That's right. He's got a bad heart.'

'As e?'

'Yes. He's just come out of Sully Hospital – three weeks ago.'

'Oh no. That can't be the same one. This one's fit as a fiddle – been livin ere for months...'

On the ground floor, Perkins' wife rang the caretaker's bell. After a long wait, a chain rattled and a bolt shot loose and the door opened. The caretaker was unshaven and hollow-eyed. 'Excuse us,' Perkins' wife said, 'but do you happen to know of a Mr Mallin living on the ninth floor? Tall, thin, elderly – '

'Aye. I knows him.'

'What can you tell us about him. We've just left him some groceries and stuff and – '

'Ew aven lent im any money ave ew?'

'Well, yes.'

'Ow much?'

'Well, twenty – '

The caretaker clapped a hand to his head and groaned. Just then an old woman appeared in a nearby doorway: 'Mr Mallin did you say?'

'That's right. He's got a bad heart.

'He's got *everything* wrong with him,' said the woman. 'He owed me two pound.'

'E owes everybody,' said the caretaker. 'I took pity on im when e first come ere and give im three poun. Never seen it since. But thas nothin: bloke on the top floor give im twenty poun an the blighter ad the cheek to go an ask the son for a loan of another fifteen without the father knowin. E gambles it away. Always in debt – '

'Well I *had* to have my two pound back,' said the old woman. 'I told him: that's my rent money, I've got to have that back – '

Perkins made a sudden dash for the pay-phone in the corner. He dialled the Oxford Street branch of Lloyd's Bank and gave them the number of Mallin's cheque. In less than a minute the voice on the other end informed him that the cheque had been cashed earlier in the morning. Perkins slammed down the receiver and swore.

'*Twenty pounds!*' said the old woman. 'That's a lot of money. I always remember: he was here one day – he'd been to Bingo and he'd won a hundred pounds. And this feller knew cause some woman had seen him win it. So there's this other man wants his fifteen pound back and old Mallin was trying to make out he didn't have it. Go on, this feller says, give it to him. You just won a hundred pound down the Elysium. In the end I seen him pull out a wad of notes – one hundred pounds – and peel off three fivers to give to this bloke. Just like that. *He'll* never go short, take my word – '

'I thought it was funny this mornin,' said the caretaker. 'E usually goes out bout ten o' clock – I knows everythin that goes on ere – but today e went out at nine an I thought it was funny then. To the bank e must ave been goin, see, to cash that cheque soon as they opened. *Twenty poun!* Duw, thas a lot of money. Well, ew won't see im now till bout seven o' clock or maybe later. E's out nearly all the time. Tell ew where I usually sees im, though: ew know the bettin shop down by the bus station by Clompus the antique dealer? Well, thas where e goes. Always in there. An then e as is meals in Belli's the fish an chip shop on the corner. Ew want to watch im. E's a fly one e is.'

'He owes Mrs Carpenter 60p,' said the old woman, 'And she's as poor as a church mouse, poor dab.'

Early that evening Perkins stood on the landing opposite number

9B Talfryn Court, reading a cheap paperback edition of the selected poems of Emily Dickinson which he'd snatched at random from a bookcase before leaving the house. He was half reading, half looking out the window. Down below, on a small triangle of grass, kids were playing tag, dodging in and out of the parked cars in the gathering dusk. The window was half open and he could hear their shouts.

Far away over the smoking rooftops he could just make out the dark smudge of sea, the hump of Kilvey Hill, and the tiny pointing finger of the Mental Hospital tower. Occasionally, there was the rumble of one or other of the lifts – the clatter of doors – feet – a key turning in a lock – the upward or downward rumble of the lift. Ronny Jones, a kid he knew from School, stopped off at his floor and said 'Ello, sir,' before disappearing into 9D. Perkins kept looking down at the street and losing his place – reading the same verse, two, three times and still not grasping the meaning. It was nearly dark. The door of 9A opened and the girl he had left the groceries with earlier on came out with the cardboard box and went to knock on 9B.

'Excuse me,' Perkins said. 'I'll take that. I've got to wait for him anyway.' He took the box from her and laid it down at his feet. He screwed up the note they'd written and tossed it out of the window.

For a long time nothing happened. He tried sitting on the box to read, then crouching and finally standing again. All of a sudden there was a commotion in 9E. The door opened and out rode a little boy on a tricycle. He collided with the wall inches from where Perkins stood and rebounded into Mallin's door: 'Look at *me!*' he yelled, 'I can fall off! I can fall off!' He capsized the tricycle still sitting on it, righted himself and throttled forward into the box of groceries. 'What you got in there?' he said. 'You got *pop*, you ave!'

Just then a woman's voice shrieked from the depths of 9E and the little boy did a three point turn and zoomed back into the flat, the door slamming shut behind him.

Perkins moved the box closer to the wall and felt something wet and sticky on his fingers. It was blood. He felt on his hands for a cut, but there wasn't one. There were more splashes on the concrete. He dug down in the box of groceries and his fingers met the ruptured bag of lamb's liver. He lifted it out gingerly and placed it on top of the faggots and eggs. Then he smeared his hands on the wall behind him and carried on reading the same verse of the same poem for the fifth time.

The shouts of the children down below had died away by now. Perkins looked out at the amber and white lights of the Town stretching away into the night and wondered if it was possible that someone somewhere else – in all that vast metropolis, in all that infinite space – could also be waiting at that very instant, in identical circumstances, alone on a cold dark landing, for someone else's return...

Ronny Jones came out of 9D and said 'Evenin, sir,' again, before pressing for the lift. Two girls came out of 9A, eyed him up and down and giggled while they also waited for the lift. When it arrived, a young man – a student, by his scarf and duffle coat – got out and knocked on Mallin's door.

'He's not in,' Perkins said.

The student glanced down at the box of groceries and leant against the wall next to Perkins. They both leaned there in silence, Perkins reading his book and the student staring darkly out at the night. They listened together for the lift's coming and going, both starting forward as the doors opened and then leaning back again as a stranger walked past and disappeared into one or other of the flats.

The caretaker came panting up the stairs. 'Still waitin for im?' he said. 'Gone to the Elysium e as – Bingo.' He crossed to the window and pointed up the street: 'Thas the way ew wanna look. Thas where e gess off the bus. Ew woan see im now till alf past ten, though. Always the same. Out in all weathers. Never in. Well, I lent im that three quid once an I never ad it back. The week after, e was askin me for 20p for the bus an like a fool I give it twim. Are ew sure thas enough I said cause, as you knows, e looks alf starved. Ew bet ter give me another 20p then e said, jus in case. Never ad it back. No. Never. I cun kiss that goodbye. E plays on ew sympathy, see. Eve borrowed money off nearly evryone. We've ad the CID up ere twice, nosin aroun – '

The student looked at his watch and dashed down the stairs.

'Mind ew, is the women are the worst trouble-makers roun ere,' continued the caretaker. 'Ew never aves no trouble with the men – but the *women!* Funny innit? But like I say: thas where I always sees im is down by the Criterion. I tell ew why: cause sometimes I goes in the Dillwyn in Union Street an there's that Bookmaker's next to Belli's fish an chip shop – Joe Coral's. E's always in there. Thas where ew'll find im. If ew wanna catch im in, though, best day's always a Sunday. Nowhere to go then, see – so e's in nearly all the time. But to tell ew the onest, I doan think e'll be ere much longer. Eve only ever paid is rent twice. Always goes out alf an our before the rent man comes roun. Thas ow e is, see – sharp.'

The caretaker left by the lift. After a few minutes the student returned and started banging on the door of 9B. 'He's *in there!*' he said. 'There's a light on in his room. I've just been outside to have a look – !'

'No he's not,' Perkins said. 'You forgot to exclude the ground floor. I nearly made the same mistake myself. You were looking at the eighth floor – the floor below us.'

The student looked gob-smacked. Perkins picked up the cardboard box and wearily pressed for the lift. 'Well, I don't know about you,' he said, 'but I've hung around long enough. I've got a wife and two kids to get home to.'

The lift doors opened and the student followed him inside. 'He's probably left the country by now, anyway,' Perkins said. 'This could be a job for Interpol.' The student didn't respond, but glowered in one corner of the lift like a caged animal. At the front entrance they went their separate ways: the student on foot in the direction of Town, Perkins to his car. He put the box on the passenger seat, started the engine and drove once round the block. When he came back, there was no sign of the student.

Back on the ninth floor, Perkins leant once more against the wall close to the stains of congealed lamb's blood and took out his Dickinson. He'd give her one last try, but she wasn't his cup of tea at all. Too cerebral by far. He wished he'd brought Catullus or Clare or anyone but her. It was going to be a long night.

Acute

Acute was on the second floor. Perkins and his father took the lift, separating when they got out: one taking the left-hand turning, the other the right. The place hadn't changed much in two years, except that the corridors seemed quieter and gloomier and almost completely deserted. Perkins found his brother first: three quarters the way along one of the other Wings, in a side Ward. It was mid-afternoon. There were two others in with him: a man stretched out asleep by the window and another sitting up in bed surrounded by visitors. Nigel was just inside by the door, sitting down in his dressing gown, in the process of lighting his pipe. When he saw Perkins he got up and went out into the corridor to greet him.

The three of them went into the Television Room and sat down alongside the TV: Perkins in a wheelchair, his father and brother on either side. There was a slim, fair-haired young man slumped in an armchair opposite, smiling fixedly at the black and white screen where Children's Hour in Welsh seemed to be on – at near maximum volume.

Nigel didn't look any different from when Perkins had last seen him – at home, a week or two before – slightly puffier around the face perhaps and more subdued but, nonetheless, still glad to see them. Under his dressing gown were three plastic discs attached to his chest with wires leading from them to a contraption in his pyjama pocket. Perkins handed him the paperback he had brought: 'I was going to get you fags as well,' he said above the din of the TV, 'but the Hospital shop is shut. It's like a bloody morgue downstairs – '

Nigel cupped a match to the end of his pipe and said it didn't matter: he had enough tobacco to keep him going for a while.

'How're you feeling, anyway?' Perkins asked.

'Okay,' Nigel said, poking at the flame. 'They took the drip away this morning.'

'What're those plastic things for?'

Nigel shook out the match. 'They're monitoring my heartbeats,' he said. 'I don't know how. Must be down in the Office somewhere. The nurse came up just now and said one of my leads was loose. How could she tell that, I wonder?'

His father leaned across and gave him a grave look: 'You're very lucky to be here – you know that, don't you? What made you do it? You've got a lovely wife and a nice home. I don't understand you – '

Nigel rolled his eyes and indicated the young man sitting opposite. His father wasn't to be put off: 'You were very lucky they got to you in time, by all accounts. What did you want to go and do a thing like that for? You were getting along so well – ' Nigel relit his still-lit pipe and started humming to the music on the TV as though his father wasn't there. The young man in the arm chair had one eye on the screen, the other on them, the smile still fixed on his face. Huge smoke screens billowed from Nigel's pipe. Just then the Welsh programme finished and the set went silent...

'I thought you'd given up drink,' his father persisted. 'You told me you hadn't drunk for two years. Anita said you went out at nine yesterday morning and bought cider in the Off Licence. Is that right?' Nigel kept on humming. 'Is that *right?*'

'Yes.'

'Then you took all her tablets and all your own. What happened then? Did you tell them you'd taken them?'

'I suppose so. I don't know. The first thing I remember is waking up in here.'

'What time was that?'

'I can't remember.'

An announcer's voice cut in, in English, to give the time and a run-down of the afternoon's programmes. Their father sank back in his chair, momentarily at a loss. 'How long are you going to be in?' Perkins asked.

'A couple of days. Maybe out tomorrow. They haven't told me yet.'

'Stay as long as you can: you need the rest.'

'Why?' Nigel said. 'I want to get home to Anita as soon as possible – she needs me.'

'You're very foolish,' his father said. 'You've had a narrow escape this time. You don't want to rush things – '

A nurse came in and started to adjust Nigel's discs: 'They're working loose,' she said. 'I think it's because you're sweating.'

Nigel stuck out his chest to her as though receiving a medal. 'He's lucky to be here, isn't he?' his father said to her, 'after what he did – '

She carried on with her adjustments: 'I'm afraid I can't discuss that,' she said brusquely.

As soon as she'd gone, his father leaned across again: 'Anita's got troubles enough of her own. What use would you be if you went and did a thing like that again and then ended up in here?'

The young man's gaze wandered from the TV to Nigel, hanging on his answer. Nigel sucked deeply at his pipe, studying a point half way up the further wall: *'Life is an herbaceous border,'* he said. *'The best plants are always at the back.'*

'What's that supposed to mean?' his father said.

'I don't know. It just came to me,' Nigel said, feeling inside his dressing gown pockets: 'Got any change on you?' he asked Perkins. 'I want to give Anita a ring.'

Perkins handed him a one pound note and five 10p pieces. Nigel got up and went next door to phone.

'What d'you make of him?' his father said when he'd gone.

'He doesn't look any different to what he looked a couple of weeks ago,' Perkins said.

'No – I mean: in *himself*. He's in a world of his own. He's talking about going out already. What use is he going to be to anybody if he tries that again? On top of which, he's got all his in-laws staying. That must be enough to drive anyone to drink. We've got to persuade him to stay in as long as he can.'

'We'd better speak to someone about him,' Perkins said. 'Find out what's happening – '

Nigel came back in and sat down. 'No answer,' he said. 'She must have slipped over to the neighbours.'

'Listen to me, son – ' his father began, drawing himself up. Nigel groaned in anticipation of another lecture and looked the other way. ' – I'm only telling you this for your own good – ' The nurse returned with a plastic box full of dressings. 'It's happened again,' she said. 'I've had to come all the way back up from downstairs. It must be because you're sweating.' She fiddled around with his discs again – gave him two new ones – and went back out. Their father got up and followed her.

Left alone, Perkins and his brother ran out of things to say. The young man opposite concentrated wholly on the TV, Nigel puffed quietly to himself, and Perkins picked up the paperback he had brought for Nigel and started to read. In a moment their father returned, followed closely by an enormous woman in a bathrobe. She leant, breathless, in the doorway and shouted across at the young man to ask how he was. 'I feel like a soddin pin-cushion!' she said, before he could reply. 'Three injections I've ad already today, an that dirty swine of a porter jus told me a very filthy joke – stinkin it was. E ought to be ashamed of imself talkin to a married woman like that – ' She staggered across to a chair, pulled it up in front of the TV, sat down and started fiddling with the knobs. The screen immediately burst into colour. 'What appened to you?' she said to Nigel. 'You aven ad an eart attack, ave you?'

'No – an accident in the house,' Nigel replied.

'Oh, I thought you'd ad an eart attack. Whassat e's readin? A dirty book, issit?' Perkins showed her. 'Oh, I thought for a moment you was readin a dirty book. Who's that by there?'

'This is my father,' Nigel said, 'and this is my brother – '

'There's lovely blue eyes you father's got,' she said. 'Same as you. Mus be in the family. *His* eyes are brown, though,' she said, indicating Perkins, 'so e must be *the lodger's!*'

She levered herself up again, roaring with laughter at her own joke, and waddled back out. When she'd gone, Nigel started to tell them about her foiled suicide attempt of several days previous but before he could finish the story the nurse came in for a third time and told him to take off his pyjama top: his heartbeats still weren't registering properly downstairs. She peeled off the plastic discs completely, screwed them up and began wiping his chest with some swabs of cotton wool. Nigel gazed down at her hands as they worked: 'Mm – that smells nice,' he said. 'What is it?'

'Alcohol wipes,' she said.

'You mean it's for wiping away alcohol?'

'No, there's alcohol in it. That's why it feels so cold.'

This time, Perkins followed the nurse out. He caught up with her just by the lift doors. She could tell him no more than she'd just told his father, she said: Nigel would stay in that Ward until they'd dealt with his physical condition, then he'd be sent downstairs to the psychiatric Ward for the doctors there to decide what to do with next.

Perkins went to look for the toilet. The further reaches of corridor were labyrinthine dismal and dark. Some beds were empty, folded blankets neatly piled on top of them; others were inhabited: an old man with an oxygen mask over his face; a man stretched out asleep with his two blind eyes open...The toilet was large and depressing – a single pedestal set in one corner with a view, from the sink, of grass growing wild out the back. On his return, he stopped to phone his wife. Next to the telephone trolley was a pile of library books and a toy surgery game: one in which joke organs had to be removed from a joke patient without ringing a bell. The bell rang as he tentatively tried to remove a spleen. In the middle of his conversation with his wife the phone went dead. Perkins followed the lead back into the TV room where he discovered that his father's feet had inadvertently kicked the lead from the socket. His father was asleep in the wheelchair, chin on chest. Nigel was smoking his pipe and staring enigmatically into space and the young man was still grinning at the Technicolor screen, where a female voice was now singing: *'If you're happy and you know it, clap your hands!'*

Visiting Time was up. Perkins woke his father and Nigel escorted them to the end of the corridor. As they stood by the lift saying goodbye, Perkins gave him some more change for the phone and his father gave him a pound and some final, unheeded words of advice.

'Shekels! Shekels!' Nigel joked, drowning out his words, hands outstretched in supplication.

The lift doors opened and shut behind Perkins and his father. 'This is going to be the pattern from now on,' his father prophesied, gloomily, on the way down. 'We'll be back and fore here for a good few years yet – unless, of course, he makes a proper job of it next time. If you or I had taken half of what he took, we'd have been goners. If I live to be a hundred, I'll never understand him, will you?'

Back on the Ground Floor, they made their way down the corridor and out into dazzling sunlight. It was hot and stuffy in the car. They wound down the windows and drove out round the roundabout and the little ornamental pond where, Nigel had told them, the enormous woman in the bathrobe had looked like a stranded whale as she tried to drown herself in two inches of water.

The Bird: A Story

Perkins had taken the day off to write a story. It was 10a.m. He'd checked over what he'd written the night before, made a score of small changes and was just reading it through when the cat jumped up on the windowsill outside and scratched on the glass. Perkins glanced up in time to see a mottled brown object in her mouth. The cat jumped down when she saw she had his attention and Perkins got up and opened the front door for her. She bounded in with a bird in her mouth – straight down the passageway and into the kitchen. Perkins ran after her, shouting at her to drop it, but the cat dodged under the kitchen table, the bird still firmly clamped in her jaws. He had to get down on his hands and knees to shoo the cat away.

It had released the bird, which now stood stock-still under a chair, eyes open but unblinking. There were a couple of feathers lying beside it and there was a mark on its back. Still on his hands and knees, Perkins crept closer but was reluctant to pick it up. His wife called from upstairs. She was in bed with a cold and wanted to know what all the noise was about.

'The cat brought in a bird,' he called up. 'A big one. Looks like a thrush.'

'Is it dead?'

'I don't know. It's not moving. It's just standing there.'

'It must be paralysed with fright,' she called down. 'Have you put the cat out?'

Perkins went and put the cat out. He approached the kitchen cautiously in case the thing was fluttering about, but it was still standing there, eyes open, under the table. He took a closer look. Its beak was moving a bit and the mark on its back didn't look too bad: no blood or anything. He opened the window in case it was able to fly out and quickly closed it again when he remembered the cat. He got some breadcrumbs and a saucer of milk and pushed them slowly in front of the bird but it hopped awkwardly away and disappeared behind the washing machine.

The cat scratched on the window and Perkins opened it and grabbed her with two hands. He put her in the front room and shut the door. Then, very carefully, he pulled the washing machine out from one wall and pushed it sideways against the other, so that the bird had only one avenue of escape. He got a scarf from the clothes-horse and got down on his hands and knees again. It was much easier than he'd thought. The bird dodged him – once, twice, and then fell over sideways onto its back. He gripped it gently in the scarf and took it upstairs to show his wife. She didn't want to touch it either. 'Put it outside on the wall to fly,' she said.

Perkins took it round the side of the house and put it on the window sill – it jumped off, hopped down the side of the house and came to rest under a plastic Centurion tank belonging to one of the kids. It pecked him and made a hissing noise when he went for it with the scarf again, so he picked it up with his bare hands.

Back upstairs, he put it in the bath together with the bread and milk. It still wasn't hungry or thirsty and made no effort to get out. He made a little nest of toilet paper at one end of the bath but the bird stayed down the plug-hole end. He opened a window, then went back downstairs to carry on with the story. He decided to abandon the one he'd been writing and write a story about finding a bird instead. He wrote a thousand words straight off, taking the story as far as the moment when he placed the bird in the bath. Then he broke off and went back up to have another look. The bird was still in the bath with the untouched bread and milk and the toilet paper – which it wasn't lying on – and two curly grey feathers. It had shit: a teaspoonful of a creamy substance. Perkins looked at it for a while. The bird knew it was being watched. It held its head quizzically to one side. Cold air came from the window. They both waited, listening to the sounds of the Town in the distance, smelling the smells of soap and shampoo and aftershave and human urine. He went back out and closed the door quietly. Downstairs he wrote another half page. The sun came out – filling his room, dazzling on the paper, making molten silver of the sea. It was exactly twelve o' clock. His hand cast a long shadow on the paper as he wrote.

Perkins had to go shopping in the afternoon. He wanted to leave going as long as possible, at least until he'd finished the bird story. After a while, he went upstairs to have another look. The bird was still there but there were a couple more loose feathers around it now. He put a shawl down in place of the toilet paper and proffered a breadcrumb dipped in milk. The bird leapt six inches in the air, loosening several more feathers. Perkins' wife called to him from the bedroom: Had he given it anything to eat yet? He had but it wouldn't touch it. It was in the bath now.

'Well, you'd better get it out!' she called. 'It'll die of cold in there.'

'It's okay, I've put a shawl in with it.'

'Why not put the TV in with it as well,' she laughed, ' – before it dies of boredom?'

'I'll leave it a bit,' Perkins said. 'Until it re-orientates itself. Then perhaps I'll take it down the P.D.S.A.'

'I want to have a bath later,' she said. 'You better get it out.'

Perkins assured her he would – all in good time. She was suddenly hungry now, she told him and could do with a bowl of soup and a nice cup of tea. No bread with the soup.

He made them both a bowl of ham and pea soup. She didn't want any bread with hers because she was slimming. She was slimming because the night before, they'd watched an autopsy on TV. It was the first one ever to be shown. The subject was an old man of seventy. They'd taken out all his vital organs and laid them on a slab: the brain, the lungs, the heart and liver. The corpse had been ripped open right down the middle. It looked like the carcasses hanging in butchers' – only greyer. They were trying to find out exactly what had killed the old man. All the organs looked shiny and new. The surgeon sliced a piece of liver for analysis and poked around with the heart for a bit. That was the cause of the trouble: a blocked artery – probably caused by overeating. So Perkins' wife didn't want any bread with her soup. Perkins took it up to her and on his way down, looked in on the bird. It was standing on the shawl now.

Back in his room, he wrote another half page, bringing in a subject he really wanted to forget: the TV autopsy of the night before. He wasn't sure whether it was entirely relevant, but it did help to explain why his wife didn't want bread with her soup and why, incidentally, he did not butter his own thin slice.

It was half past twelve now, the sun still shining between breaks in the cloud. He went up to the bathroom to have a wash and shave.

None of the sounds of his washing seemed to perturb the bird. It remained standing on the shawl as Perkins washed and pulled the plug out, peed and flushed the toilet. His wife called again from the bedroom. She wanted to give him a shopping list. Perkins quickly combed his hair and went into her, leaving the bird still standing among the smells of Nivea cream and toothpaste and Oil of Ulay.

He was gone an hour and returned loaded with groceries – everything she'd put on the list bar the liver. The bird was on its back in the bath when he went to look. There were a lot of feathers lying around now, but it wasn't dead. He nudged it with a loofah and it righted itself and fluttered down to the plug-hole end.

His wife wanted a bath in a minute and the kids would be home soon and he'd have to make tea. 'Alright! Alright!' he said. 'Give me five minutes and I'll take it to the P.D.S.A.' He went downstairs, wrote another two hundred words and then went upstairs again. He used the shawl to get hold of the bird. As he lifted it from the bath it dropped and fluttered behind the toilet pedestal. He caught it again and took it out the front. When he let it go it hopped all the way down the steps – thirty of them – and took off from the garden wall. It fell ten feet and landed in the gutter. Perkins went after it and wrapped it gently in the shawl. He got in his car, holding it with one hand to his chest, and drove the short distance to the P.D.S.A. It was cold and beginning to rain when he got there. A pretty girl assistant was at Reception. She had small, white, delicate hands and a nice figure. She unwrapped the bird from the shawl and pulled lightly at the loose feathers on its back. They came away in a cluster. Another girl came in: 'It doesn't look too good to me,' she said. 'Perhaps the best thing would be to put it down.'

The first girl spread out the bird's wings: 'It looks like a young one. It's so thin – '

The second girl took a closer look: 'Look *there*,' she said. 'There's a hole in its head.' Perkins looked closer. He hadn't noticed the hole before.

'They usually die when they're like this,' the first girl said. 'Perhaps the best thing is for us to put it down.'

'Or else you can try and nurse it,' the second girl said. 'You could take it home for an hour and see how it goes and then bring it back down. Try feeding it Kit E Kat. We're open till five.'

'Okay,' Perkins said. 'That's what I'll do then: I'll take it home for a bit and try it on Kit E Kat.'

When he got back he told his wife he was going to put the bird in a cardboard box in his room. She was getting fed up: 'Make the kids' food,' she said. 'Liver and chips – '

'I couldn't get liver,' Perkins lied.

'Couldn't or wouldn't?' she said. 'Don't tell me you're going to get squeamish about eating liver from now on, are you?'

Perkins went and got a cardboard box for the bird. He placed it inside together with an old pullover, half a sausage and an egg cupful of water. Then he went and washed the bath out and started to get the tea ready. He checked once while the food was cooking. The bird had either eaten the sausage or was sitting on it. He put the other half in with it and tried it with a spoonful of water, but still it wouldn't drink.

When the kids came home Perkins told them what had happened. They stood wide-eyed outside his room as he warned them that if there was the slightest noise the bird would die. They tiptoed over to the cardboard box and stared in without a word.

It was early evening. Perkins' wife and kids were in the front room watching TV. Perkins had just sat down to his story when there was a movement in the box. Suddenly the bird jumped out onto the cardboard flap. It stood there for a full minute, perfectly still, as though listening. Then it jumped down on the floor. When Perkins made to get up, it ran under the sideboard. He sat back down and carried on writing. It was raining now and getting dark.

The bird had moved behind the armchair. It was a little dark ball in the shadow of his cassette holder. He didn't want to leave it in the room overnight because there were so many of his paintings and drawings lying about, so when he'd finished writing he got a plastic laundry basket – the kind with ventilation slits in the side – from the kitchen. The bird ran under the sideboard, across the room, under his desk, back to the armchair, under the sideboard, behind the bookcase, back under his desk and back to the sideboard again before he finally caught it. He put it in the basket with the pullover, sausage and eggcup of water and put a drawing board on top. Then he put the whole thing on the sideboard, out of reach of the cat.

That night the kids both said goodnight to the bird. One of them put a slice of banana in with it and the other one a bit of pear. They kept getting out of bed to come back down and have a last look. The bird wasn't moving much, but it looked comfortable enough.

The following morning it seemed to be in the same position, still with its eyes open and still alive. Perkins could see its chest slightly moving. He put some crumbs in with it and poked a spoonful of water through a slit, but it wouldn't drink. The kids got up and looked and so did his wife. They all had breakfast and then left for School and work.

In his dinner hour, Perkins drove home. He didn't have a lot of time. The bird was leaning against the bars, its body tilted forward. He poked it with a sheet of cartridge paper but it didn't move. He took the drawing board off the basket and looked inside. The bird had shit several more times. The eggcup had been tipped over and the food was untouched.

Not wanting the kids to come home and find it first, he took the laundry basket round the side of the house. There, he dug a six inch hole in the flower bed with a trowel and shovelled the bird in. Its eyes were still open. He covered it with earth and patted it down. Then he took the basket in the house, locked the front door and drove back to work.

Time Piece

Regular as clockwork, they got home at four, picked up the kids and went straight out again to do the shopping. An hour later, they returned for Perkins and the kids to unload the bags and then drove back into Town, intending to go for a meal. Outside the Pyramid Tandoori, some time around six, Perkins looked at his watch. Where it should have been was the pale-white template of watch and strap stencilled on the bare flesh. 'My *watch*,' he said. 'It's gone!'

Nobody seemed unduly concerned. 'You probably took it off in the house,' his wife said.

'No,' he said. 'I looked at it before we left Tesco's, so I had it on then.' He patted his pockets and started groping the floor of the car. It was his father's gold presentation watch, commemorating a lifetime's service to the Dock's Board. Perkins had borrowed it while his own was being repaired.

His wife felt in the glove compartment: 'Think what you've been doing this evening,' she said, 'and where you've been. Could you have left it in the house when you took the bags up?'

Owain piped up from the back seat: 'He tried to break up that old arm chair you threw out, just before we came away – '

Perkins stopped rummaging in the door pocket and thought for a moment: He'd been sick of seeing the chair lying there at the bottom of the garden, so he'd had a go at breaking it up. The watch must have come off then. They all agreed that was what had happened. His wife and kids would go to the restaurant and Perkins would return to retrieve it and follow them on.

It was mid-Autumn. He drove back in a hurry, calculating an hour of daylight still left. That would give him until – he looked, instinctively, at his wrist…

His wife had unceremoniously dumped the armchair in the garden several days before. She'd been on at Perkins for some time to get rid of it. It was over thirty years old – early CO-OP, the last survivor of a hand-me-down suite from his in-laws – but, even so, very comfortable and the only one in his studio that Perkins had ever really been able to relax in. Earlier that evening, as he'd been leaving the house for the second time, he'd been seized by the impulse to rip it apart to see what unsuspected treasures had accumulated inside. Axe-less, he'd bashed away at it with a convenient brick and felt, with his watch hand, down its back and sides.

It was still lying on its back where he'd left it. He looked first where he remembered looking previously, inserting a hand into the torn stuffing, carefully feeling, pulling away clutch after clutch of wool and horse hair. Then he searched the ground. It was strewn with stones and bits of brick and leaves from the old sycamore. He foraged about all round the chair, then set it upright and looked underneath. Nothing. He ripped off the fabric backing to reveal the coarse sacking and the metal springs and groped down the back again, stretching his fingers while simultaneously craning over the top of the chair to see if they would emerge. Physically impossible. Perched where he was, he looked as though he was trying to make love to the chair. He insinuated his hand further along, wary of how, with its twin some years before, his finger had encountered a needle. There was no needle in this one, though: no needle, no coins, no key, no toy soldiers, pencil, crayon, pen – no gold presentation watch.

Suddenly, he had a brain-wave. He pressed his ear close to the seat and listened. Moving slowly around, he listened to the arms, back, front, underside. He listened to the chair all over but: nowhere a tell-tale pulse of cogs or a single breath left in it. A spider ran over the exposed woodwork. He picked up a piece of brick and flicked it away. A second spider appeared and disappeared and somewhere, perversely, an insect ticked. The sky was getting dark: two or three tones darker than when he started. He straightened up and looked out to sea, his back stiff from crouching, one leg gone almost to sleep. Soon it would be lighting up time. He looked at his wrist…

Where else: on who else's wrist, in who else's pocket could his father's gold presentation watch be ticking now? How could they know its value, envisage the particular and unique time it had ticked away? He stood in the spilt guts of chair blanking out the night, trying to retrace his footsteps:

…hands at his sides, he enters Tesco's… passes the fruit and veg and flowers and frozen food…stops to look at a felt-tip pen on offer – decides against it, wanders on to the books and magazines, the tapes and videos…his wife calls: where's he *been*? Has she got to do it all? *'Push the trolley!'* He pushes the trolley as she selects and loads, stopping interminably, dropping in this and that, occasionally changing her mind, replacing, substituting, the end of one aisle, down another: cooking foil…cat-food…dog-food…Domestos…Vim…bog-paper…*Bread!* She must remember bread: wholemeal for her because she's slimming, white for the kids…up one aisle down another…momentous decisions: which cheese, which bag of spuds, which cut of bacon?…*Which hand is pushing the trolley now? What is the left hand doing? What is the sensation at the wrist?*…he buys pretzels: his watch hand reaching to the shelf and down to the trolley…on then to the breakfast cereals, to the soft drinks – and the booze. He stops for a long, lingering moment, inspecting the shiny ranks of bottles – and then they're in the queue. He fetches a cardboard box…he loads the box as the conveyor belt rolls down the goods…the box is full, he staggers to the car…*Nowhere the sound of anything dropping, nowhere the sensation of release…*

Evening. A ship in the Bay. A dog barking behind rooftops, the lighthouse flickering at the tip of the peninsula. The chair lying – a stricken wrestler, a lost lover – at his feet. He shakes it one last time, punches it so that the springs twang. The chair lies damply still under the approaching stars. He can hear a leaf fall, a gnat's wings whirr. Clouds pass heavy overhead, milky-white with rain. He dreams of the watch in the ground still ticking and then in twenty-four hours not ticking and then in thirty years or three hundred the garden finally excavated and the watch, more green than golden, found.

Street lights come on but still he stands. Soon he'll pick up the family, appetites sated, all of them wondering where he's been. When they get home, Owain will ask for the key to the car so he can have one last look and Perkins will sigh hopelessly as he hands it over: *'It's no use – it's gone for good.'* And then five minutes later Owain will rush in and, to everyone's astonishment, place the watch on the kitchen table and say: *'I found it. It was down the side by the handbrake all the time.'*

Tomorrow night, Perkins will set fire to the chair. Starting with a clutch of hair and leaves – the kids watching from the bedroom window – thick white smoke billowing upward, flame eating into the stuffing, biting towards the wood. He'll stand back in the cool shadows mesmerized, eyes flickering with fire, seeing himself consumed, seeing his wife and himself making furious love consumed, and all the lovers and dreamers the chair had ever held burn, and all the long-lost evenings blazing up in savage ecstasy. And in the morning he'll come to poke the ashes, sift among the blackened castors and springs and screws, his father's gold watch warm and vibrant on his wrist in the early light.

Fixture

Just home from work, Perkins was tired out and ready for his tea. He'd barely been slumped two seconds in his favourite armchair when Mathew came in and told him he had a rugby game on – his first one ever for the school team. Perkins groaned: 'Where?'

'Cwmherbert – I think.'

'Where the hell's *Cwmherbert?*'

His son didn't know.

'What time's kick-off?'

He didn't know that either.

'Have they laid on transport?'

Mathew shook his head: he didn't think so. A pained look came over Perkins' face: 'You don't know where, you don't know when, you don't know how – '

'We've got to meet at the Club House, first.' Mathew said quickly. 'Four thirty, I think.'

'You *think!*'

Perkins' wife came in and told Perkins not to be so grumpy and to take the boy. 'Alright,' he said, 'but I'm not being grumpy – I *want* to take him. I'd go to the ends of the earth to see his first game – if only I knew where it was and when it started.'

They reached the Club House bang on four thirty. Mathew went in to find out what was happening. Kick-off was at five o' clock at Cwmherbert, according to a boy he'd seen, but the boy thought everyone had gone. Perkins looked at his watch: 'It's four thirty five now,' he said. 'We'd better go home. If we knew where Cwmherbert was, it'd be something, but we don't even know that – or if we'd get there in time. Cwmherbert must be a long way away – I *know* it's nowhere round here. You better give this one a miss.'

Mathew's eyes started to fill up. Just then two of his friends appeared with kit bags and asked for a lift. The kick-off was at six o' clock and they knew the way.

It was a thirty minute run. On the way Perkins brightened up a bit, even discussing tactics – demonstrating the finer points of the hand-off using Mathew, in the passenger seat, as a dummy.

The pitch was situated in a deep valley just off the main road. It looked small and churned up. The home team, supposedly all under thirteen, had been changed and waiting for forty minutes. They were hanging around outside the changing room jumping up and down to try and keep warm. The rest of Mathew's team and their Coach arrived in several car-loads and they all went in together to change. Cwmherbert came out first – a forbidding black and blue – to the cheers of the local supporters. They looked uniformly big – flinging the ball about with confidence, catching and kicking like veterans. The Whites followed – all shapes and sizes, well-laundered but mostly small, Mathew suddenly frail and vulnerable by comparison. Perkins jumped out of the car and followed them onto the field. Mathew stopped at the touchline. His nose was red, his eyes were already watering with the cold and he was shivering. 'Go on!' Perkins said, slapping him on the back, 'get out there and give em *hell!*'

Mathew shook his head: 'No, Dad – I'm substitute.'

'*Substitute!*' Perkins stifled an oath. 'Don't tell me we've come all this way and you're not even playing – ' Mathew started running on the spot, jumping up and down, and slapping his sides. 'Go and get a coat on then,' Perkins said. 'You can't wait about like that. It's bloody perishing out here.' Mathew obediently trotted back the way he'd come. *'We're one short!'* came a shout from the field. All the players looked towards the small figure making for the changing rooms. *'Who's that over there?'* the Whites' Coach shouted. *'Where the hell's* he *going!'* He called after Mathew and Mathew turned and ran red-faced onto the far wing. He looked even smaller now.

The whistle went: twenty minutes each way, kick-off to Cwmherbert. Play swung erratically back and fore but mostly fore towards the Whites' line. Two quick tries to the Black and Blues. Perkins wished he'd brought his glasses: Mathew – was it Mathew? – was swallowed up in a melée far out. The ball came back to the Black and Blues…along the line…out to the wing…the Whites weren't tackling. Where was Mathew? **'It im ard! It im ard!'** the Whites Coach shouted, striding up the line, a fag wedged in his mouth. Try number three...the Black and Blues began to hit their stride – started to play exhibition stuff, taking it in turns to make a break. There was Mathew, still out there on the wing, small and grey in the gathering dusk, advancing and retreating – inexorably falling back. **'Tackle low!'** the Whites Coach shouted but the Whites wouldn't tackle high or low.

Half time. Sixteen – nil, approximately, to the Black and Blues. The Whites re-grouped, dazed and worn. The Coach stamped on his fag and gave them a verbal hammering: 'Look at his jersey,' he said, singling out a forward. 'Not one tackle. Not *one* bloody tackle. It's *diabolical*! That ball isn't bloody hot **– pick it up!'**

Second half. Mathew was ordered to the other wing, so he was still just as far away. Onslaught on onslaught of black and blue... Perkins strolled around to the other side of the pitch. It was getting very dark now: lights on in the houses, the mountain dissolving into sky. **'It im ard! It im ard!'** from the Club House side...a kick...a slither and slide of bodies...touch. 'Get them *low!*' Perkins heard himself shout. 'Round the *legs!*'...Loose maul from the line-out...a kick ahead...charge...muffled tackle...pushover try to them. The floodlights came on: three 60 watt bulbs on poles, making a snowball-in-hell's difference. Another try...and another. Final whistle. **'Three cheers for the visitors!'...'Three cheers for Cwmherbert – !'** fading away into the darkness. Pats on the back, handshakes, hugs, commiserations – the slow drift back to the changing rooms. 'Never mind, boys,' – the Whites' Coach, philosophical, lighting up – 'it was a run-out...'

Perkins waited in the car, listening to the radio. There was a musical panel game on. One team had to name the sixteen choristers on a record made by a famous choir Perkins had never heard of. They named about ten. When was the performance given? 'Fifth of October 1938.' Correct. One of the singers was, of course, now a Dame. 'I saw her the other day,' said a panellist. 'She looks marvellous. Hasn't changed a bit.' Cars started up and left. Groups dispersed, frosty-breathed into the night. Perkins turned the radio down low not to waste the battery. The pitch was getting darker and darker – nearly black as the floodlights went out.

His wife was watching TV when they got back. Their food was in the kitchen and they were to eat it out there because she was on a diet and couldn't bear to watch anyone else stuffing. They ate their food and went into the living room. There was a programme on about Einstein and his Theory of Relativity. In the vicinity of a Black Hole time slows down and eventually stops. If the earth got sucked into a Black Hole it would be reduced to a circumference of one inch. If you travelled away from earth at the speed of light and returned in a day, hundreds of years would have passed on earth. Space is so vast that everything that has ever happened on earth has probably already happened and will probably happen again on identical planets somewhere else in the universe. Everything in the universe that is built up must eventually be broken down. On the moon a feather and a hammer dropped simultaneously land at the same time. Perkins fell asleep in the chair. He woke up stretched out on the settee – alone. The blinds were drawn, the gas fire and the light were still on and the dog was curled up on the mat. He didn't know where he was for a moment or what time it was. He thought it must be morning but his watch told him: quarter past midnight. He fed the cat and the dog and went up to bed. His wife was sleeping. He undressed quickly, picked up a book, got into bed, read three paragraphs and realised he'd seen an adaptation of it before on TV. It was the hundredth anniversary, almost to the day, of the birth of Albert Einstein – a Piscean, like himself. He put the book down, switched off the light and closed his eyes.

The Blue Bird of Happiness on a Plate

1

Early on the morning after his mother died, Perkins went to call on his father. He expected to find him still in bed, but he was already up and at the kitchen sink, sleeves rolled, washing some dishes.

He felt alright he said. He'd had a reasonable night's sleep, three cold fish fingers from the fridge and a cup of tea for breakfast: 'I'm doing exactly what I normally do,' he said. 'Got up at the same time, made the bed, saw to the stove, washed, shaved, had breakfast and, as soon as I've finished these few things, I'm going to change and get the car out of the garage. Sit down and have a read of the paper – '

Perkins went into the front room with the previous day's Express and sat down by the television. The blinds were not drawn and although the room was normally dim-lit, light flooded in from the street. He sat looking at himself on the cold grey screen, sitting in the chair she'd sat in just before she went to fetch the coal, looking over the top of the Express while his father padded about somewhere overhead…

They drove East along the winding Valley road to break the news to Perkins' brother who lived an hour's drive away on a Council estate near Pontypridd. They didn't say much. Perkins' father concentrated on his driving and Perkins sat staring out of the window, rehearsing what he was going to say and how best to say it.

'There's a piece of paper in my top pocket,' his father said after a mile or two. 'Have a look at it and see what you think.' Perkins reached across and took the piece of paper from his father's breast pocket. Written on it, in copperplate handwriting was:

PERKINS - suddenly on May 1st at 73 Llewellyn Terrace, Fairfield, Alma

>beloved wife of Cliff, mother of
>Alvin and Nigel and Grandmother of
>Sarah, David, Lyn, Mathew and Owain.
>Funeral arrangements later.

'How does it sound?' his father said, eyes still fixed on the road.
'Okay' Perkins said.
'There's two e's in 'arrangements', isn't there?'
'I think you can spell it with one or two.'
'What about the punctuation – is that alright?'
'Fine,' Perkins said, replacing the piece of paper.
'I'm going to pop it in on the way back. It'll be in the Evening Echo tomorrow. One night – that's enough, isn't it?'
Perkins nodded. 'What about finances?' he said. 'D'you want to borrow any money?'
'It's only 60p for one night.'
'No – I don't mean that. I mean have you got enough to pay for everything. The funeral and all that.'
'Oh yes,' his father said. 'I've had that put by for a long time. Enough to bury Alma *and* me if necessary.'

Nigel was curled up fast asleep on a settee when they arrived and was still groggy when Perkins broke the news. He sat back down on the settee, waxen-pale, fully dressed but for his shoes and one sock. The kids were all in school and Anita had gone to her mother's for the day. His father handed him a carrier-bag full of old, cast-off shirts and pullovers which he'd been saving for him. 'Shall I make a cup of tea?' he suggested. 'You've had a nasty shock.'
'I'll do it,' Nigel said.
'No – I will,' Perkins said. He went out the kitchen and put the kettle on. While he was searching for cups and saucers he could hear his father giving a discreetly abridged version of how he'd come home to find the TV on and Alma's body outside by the coal shed. 'I'm not a bit surprised this has happened,' he kept saying, 'the way she's been running about of late. I've told her time and time again. She must have been just going to top up the stove be-

fore she went out – '

Nigel was rolling a cigarette from a tobacco tin when Perkins returned with the tea. 'And funny thing,' he said, biting a strand of tobacco from the thin little fag, 'I was going to phone her last night – I always phone her on a Tuesday, but for some reason, last night I didn't – ' He lit the fag with a shaking hand and the whole thing shrivelled to practically nothing. 'I'll have to buy a suit then,' he said, ' – And what about a wreath?'

'Don't worry about the wreath,' his father said. 'I'll see to that – and you can pay me when you've got it.'

'And you can borrow one of my suits,' Perkins said.

Nigel took a last puff at the fag and flicked it into the grate. 'I'll have to tell Anita and the kids now,' he said. 'They'll be upset. They thought the world of Alma.'

'We're all going to miss her,' his father sighed, 'there's no doubt about that.'

'And what about you? What are you going to do now, Dad?' Nigel said. 'You can come and live with us if you like.'

His father shook his head: absolutely no way did he want to live with anyone else. He just wanted to carry on as he'd been doing all along. Except, of course, that Alma wouldn't be there…He reached in his breast pocket: 'By the way: this is what I'm putting in the Echo,' he said. 'See if it's alright.'

Nigel held the piece of paper in his hand and stared at it for a moment: 'Fine,' he said.

'One night – that's alright, isn't it?'

'Should be.'

They finished their tea and their father collected the three cups and took them out to the kitchen to wash. 'How's he been taking it?' Nigel asked while he was gone.

'Alright,' Perkins said. 'But I don't think it's sunk in with him yet.'

Their father returned from the kitchen. They had to go now, he told Nigel: there were things to be done. Nigel got up and saw them to the door. He couldn't come out he said because he had nothing on his feet. Perkins gave him a pound and so did his father.

'How d'you think he took it?' his father asked as they drove away from the Estate.

'Alright,' Perkins said.

'I don't know so much,' his father said, 'I don't think it's sunk in with him yet – '

On the way back Perkins and his father called in the Echo Offices with the notice. The afternoon was spent receiving calls, receiving callers, making tea, making arrangements, finding and getting and filling in the necessary forms and certificates. The phone and the door bell hardly stopped ringing, the kettle whistled non-stop. Everyone seemed to have a memory and a story to tell about Alma and her final hours.

Then, suddenly the house was empty again. It was mid-evening, shadows already darkening across the lawn, the room in semi-twilight. His father didn't put the light on. He sat down at the kitchen table in his shirt sleeves with the two halves of a broken pair of women's glasses in his hand and a small screwdriver.

There were two or three specks of dried blood on one lens. Slowly and methodically, as Perkins had seen him work a thousand times before, dismantling stoves and fires and wirelesses, he removed the two small screws that held the plastic arms. He pocketed the arms, crossed to the stove with the two eye pieces and removed the lid: 'These are no good now,' he said. Perkins jumped up from the table: 'No! I'll keep them – ' He took them from his father and put them in his pocket.

His father replaced the lid and sat back down at the table. He looked up the garden, drumming his fingers lightly on the table. 'Did you have last night's Echo, Alvin?' he said after a bit.

'No. Did you?'

'No.'

'Dispute again?'

'Must be.' His fingers broke into a light canter. 'They said that was over, though.'

'Must have flared up again.'

'Must have.' The sound of hooves faded into the darkness. 'Listen, Alvin,' his father said. 'I've been thinking of cancelling my Echo. There's no point in us both getting it. Do you think you could keep yours for me – when they start back again, that is?'

'Okay,' Perkins said. 'There's bugger all in it, anyway...'

2

'Surname?'
'Perkins.'
'Christian names?'
'Alma, Victoria.'
'Date of birth?'
'Five, three, o four.'
'Place of birth?'
'Bristol.'

Sleeves rolled up, pencil wedged behind his ear, the beefy Coroner slammed out the letters on his tiny typewriter, manhandling the flimsy carriage back and fore.

Perkins and his father sat on a bench, his father intermittently calling out the requisite information. It was a new Police Station – all glass and brick – situated on the outskirts of Town. From where they were, in a little office somewhere on the third floor, they could look out through a large plate-glass window and see cows lazily munching on the adjacent hill. Not yet 10 o' clock, the sun was blazing in a blue, cloudless sky. The sound of stammering typewriters wafting faintly along the maze of corridors formed a persistent undertone to the Coroner's loud hammering.

'CAUSE OF DEATH,' he said finally, lining up his margin: *'Massive Coronary.'* He ripped the two sheets from the carriage and handed the top copy to Perkins' father who folded it up neatly and placed it in his inside coat pocket.

'Massive Coronary,' he said as they walked along the same corridor for the third time, trying to find their way out. 'I'd rather it was

that than for the fall to have killed her – '

3

Friday morning, without telling his wife, Perkins went to a second-hand bookshop in Town and bought a remaindered copy of his first book for 15p. It had been marked down from 75p to 35p but when he came to pay, the assistant flicked through the pages and said he could have it for 15p.

He drove to the Chapel of Rest in Frog Street, circled it twice, and parked further on, on the other side of the road. He opened the book and searched through his pockets for something to write with. Eventually, he found a short stub of pencil in the glove compartment and, after a moment's thought, scribbled a brief message on the fly leaf.

The Chapel was an ugly-looking building of mock Tudor design with shop-sized frosted windows downstairs. A burly, flat-capped man, who looked as though he'd been crying, was just coming away. Perkins waited a while, then wandered over. A man with a black moustache and off-white hair yellowing around the sides, answered the door. 'My mother is lying in rest here, I believe,' Perkins said.

'What is the name, please?'

'Perkins.'

The man nodded: 'Yes, that's right. Won't you come in – '

'I don't want to view the body,' Perkins quickly explained. 'But I've brought a book– '

'Take a seat, please, Mr Perkins,' said the man. 'I won't be a moment.' He went out through a rear door, leaving Perkins alone in the little office. There was a lot of paperwork on the desk and a Daily Mail on top open at the Racing page. Sunlight streamed down through the top windows, which were not frosted, casting rectangles of light on the far walls. In a minute the man returned. 'Would you like to come this way, please,' he said.

Perkins stood up: 'I don't want to see her,' he said.

'But perhaps you would care to view the coffin – '

Perkins followed him along a short passageway which led to another room. It was wood-panelled and bare and full of rows of chairs. There were three coffins: one down either side and one in front of a kind of altar.

'There,' said the man, motioning with his arm. 'I'll leave you alone for a few minutes, Mr Perkins.' He went quietly out and closed the door behind him...

Perkins' wife was making the dinner when he got back. Up to her eyes in it at the stove: saucepan bubbling away, transistor blaring, washing machine at full blast, spin dryer gone berserk and the room misty with steam. She glanced up as he came in: 'What's the matter with you?' she said. 'You look as though you've been crying.'

'I went down the Chapel,' he said, flopping down on a chair. 'Not to see her. Just to leave one of my books. I asked the bloke if he'd put it in the coffin.'

'Which book was it?'

'Poetry. The first one I had published.'

His wife strained a saucepan into the sink, plonked it on the draining board and smiled: 'I think Alma would have preferred a good Agatha Christie,' she said.

The table was laid for five. His father stood in the middle of the kitchen: 'What do you think of these?' he said to Perkins.

'What do I think of what?'

'The shoes. They look alright, don't they?'

He was wearing a pair of flat, brown, tightly-fitting lace-up shoes which looked like a woman's.

'They're okay, I suppose.'

'A pair of Alma's,' he said. 'Pity to throw them out – and they fit perfectly.'

He sat down at the table. There were a lot of clothes down the house that Perkins' wife could have, he said: 'a sheepskin coat and a few other things. They're no good to me. You can come and get them whenever you like. And there's a pile of oil paints and stuff up in the back bedroom, too, you can – ' He closed his eyes in mid-sentence and held a hand to his face. The two boys exchanged bemused glances and stared at their grandfather. Perkins' wife placed a steaming-hot plate of food in front of him and one in front of Perkins: 'Don't worry about things like that now, Cliff,' she said. 'There'll be plenty of time to sort that out later.'

'I had a letter from the Boss this morning,' Perkins said chirpily, stabbing at a potato. 'What a laugh! "Dear Mr Perkins, I write *formally* to extend the sympathies of your colleagues – " *Formally!* It's a wonder he hadn't put "Dear Sir" or "To whom it may concern".'

His father wiped his eyes. 'I had some nice letters,' he said. 'One from Councillor Mason and another from Mrs Brunswick and one from the Fairfield Police. People have been calling in all morning. They're going to miss Alma, there's no doubt about that.' He picked up his fork. 'Rosebud Browne has written a poem about her,' he said. 'She gave me a copy. She wants to send it to the Echo – but I don't want that. Alma wouldn't want it either.'

'What's it like?'

'You know the sort of stuff Rosebud writes. Well-meant but very soppy and sentimental – all about how wonderful Alma was and how much she'd done for Fairfield. All that sort of thing.'

'You'll have to tell her then,' Perkins said.

'I know. But I don't want to hurt her feelings.'

'Just say: thank you for the poem, Rosebud – you'll always treasure it, but you'd rather she didn't sent it to the Echo. She'll understand.'

His father put down his fork. And then the Residents' Association were talking about starting a fund to have a seat put by the bowling pavilion in Warmley Park with Alma's name on it. But he knew *that* wouldn't come to anything. That was all talk. People said things at the time they didn't really mean. It was just soft soap.

Perkins' wife brought her plate over and sat down next to Owain. 'Oh, I don't know,' she said. 'Alma did a lot for Fairfield. Perhaps they really will do it.'

His father smiled and shook his head. No they wouldn't. It was human nature. That idea would just die a death. Once you were gone, you were soon forgotten.

Perkins and his wife exchanged glances. His father was silent for a moment blowing lightly on his plate, dispersing the steam. 'Funny thing,' he said. 'I had a dream about Alma last night. I was in the garden – Alma was somewhere about – when I heard this plane engine overhead: a humming sort of sound. Suddenly it cut out. I was expecting to hear it start up again but it had cut out completely. I looked up to see where it was but there was thick cloud about. Then after a moment, there it came – down out of the clouds, in three pieces. In one part was a girl with a crash helmet on and all the flying gear.'

'What happened then?' Perkins asked.

'I don't know. I woke up.'

'That's odd,' Perkins' wife said. 'Alvin had a dream about Alma, too.'

'Yes,' Perkins said. 'She was coming along by Fairfield Cross and I was coming the other way. "Can't stop," she said, "I've *got* to get home. I *must* hurry." I tried to make her walk but she rushed on ahead of me – weaving her way through all the traffic to cross the road. Wouldn't listen to me.'

His father sighed. 'I know,' he said. 'That was your mother all over. She never could take her time. *Always* had to do things in a hurry.'

4

Perkins lay perfectly still, feet together, arms at his sides, chin resting on the fold of the sheet, staring out at the Bay, counting the seconds between the lightship's flashes, imagining the bed to be a raft and the rooftops a gentle causeway down to the deep…

He knew she was awake, could sense it in the slight tension of her body next to his, but he carried on mutely counting: seven… seven…thirteen…seven…seven…thirteen…

'By the way, Alvin,' she said suddenly. 'You'll have to tell your father about those shoes – '

He swivelled his head: 'What about them?'

'He looks bloody daft in them. It's not the best of ways to keep your mother's memory alive.'

'What's wrong with that?' he said. 'If he wants to wear them, I don't see why not. He's not hurting anyone – '

'Yes, but if he goes out like that. And that jumper he had on – I'm sure that was one of Alma's. Tell him – for his own sake. He'll be wearing her knickers next.'

'OK,' Perkins said. 'If you say so. I'll drop him a gentle hint tomorrow: "Dad, take Alma's shoes off – you look *bloody ridiculous* in them – "'

'You know what I mean,' she said. '*Tell* him – for his own sake…'

5

As people started to arrive, Perkins went up the garden. He wandered round behind the greenhouse, potching around, exploring the two ancient Anderson shelters that were there. They were cobwebbed and rusty and full of all sorts of junk his father couldn't bring himself to throw out: odd cuts of wood, parts of defunct machinery: a grass-catcher off a mower, bits off a bike and a Lambretta, broken garden tools – even a couple of his old toy soldiers and Dinky cars. He picked up a red plastic gun that fired suction-tipped darts and was surprised to find that it was loaded. He pointed it in the direction of an apple tree and pulled the trigger. It had a very powerful spring-release action that fired the dart with a loud twang. He strolled over to where the dart landed, picked it up out of the grass and reloaded. From where he now was, on the top lawn, he could see down through the kitchenette and living room. Shadowy figures were moving about and at that moment the front door was being opened and more people admitted. This time he fired the dart in the air to see how high it would go. It soared away above the line-post and the apple tree, arced and fell. He tried it again – and again: *Twang!* upward into the dazzling white…over… and down. *Twang! Twang! Twang!* In a next-door upstairs window shaving, Mr Darlington, a good friend of his mother's was watching him. Perkins dropped the gun and strolled casually back up behind the greenhouse. He stayed there for as long as he felt he decently could, then went back indoors.

More flowers had arrived, so many now he had a job stepping over them all. They seemed to be everywhere: on the draining board, sink, floor, fridge, even across the top of the stove. His father wanted a list kept as they arrived – all the names and all the messages – and had given Nigel the job. Soon there was no space left inside, so they had to lay some on the back steps and on the flower bed. He went back into the front room, which was now quite crowded: people in dark best clothes standing awkwardly against walls or sitting stiffly in chairs, on stools, holding subdued conversation. He latched on to an elderly neighbour who looked lost and, for some reason, they stood talking about the man's elder son's experiences on the Imjin River In the Korean War. *'She was one of the kindest persons I've ever met,'* he overheard an invalid Aunt telling his brother, *'…heart of gold…'* He drifted from the neighbour, who now looked even more lost, to his retired ex-Merchant Navy Uncle Billy whom he'd last bumped into six years previous in the Underground toilet near High Street Station. Now, after the initial greetings and handshake all he could think of for an opener was to ask about his Uncle's hiatus hernia which, he knew from his father, had remained untreated for years. It wasn't a subject his Uncle Billy wanted to be reminded of and it became obvious from his flushed expression and slightly slurred responses, that he'd had a couple of stiffeners before coming.

Perkins wandered into the parlour where Elsie, the home help and Mrs Withers were putting the finishing touches to a table full of sandwiches. He thanked them for all they'd done and drifted back out again.

The minister arrived and the service started. There were people standing outside in the kitchen and in the parlour. He stood by the front door next to the barometer, head unbowed, concentrating hard on not listening to the words. *'Life is not the candle, it's the flame,'* said the minister. Nigel reached in the pocket of his outsize waistcoat, pulled out a pair of sunglasses and put them on. The Aunt started to cry – great stifled sobs shaking her whole arthritic body and the chair she sat in. Perkins stared at the oil painting on the wall: a copy of a Hobbema: an avenue of trees somewhere in France, painted from a picture postcard. He imagined himself walking away up the narrowing thread of road, past the steepled church – whose perspective had been all wrong until she'd got him to correct it for her – over the horizon and into the blue distance.

6

Liz would have to come and pick out what she wanted, his father said, opening the wardrobe door to display an array of clothes. He closed it again and turned the key. It was mid June and the sun was still shining. 'This bedroom's exactly the same as it was the day Alma died – I haven't touched a thing,' he said. 'I won't sleep in here again and nobody else will either. At least, not in my life time – ' He went back downstairs and left Perkins to it.

The back bedroom smelt of oil paint and damp. This had been Perkins' room. Ten feet by five, it hadn't changed much in eighteen years. It had been built onto the original house by some cowboy builders a few years before they'd moved in and they'd always had insulation problems with it. In summer it had been like an oven; in winter tiny icicles formed on the ceiling.

Here he'd spent interminable hours slogging away over Latin and Algebra and the odd Health and Efficiency. Here he'd written his first poem and had his first wet dream.

Now, although his father had tiled the ceiling and wood-panelled the walls and it still had a single bed, it was used mainly as a store room. There was an old oil heater in there, an electric fire and an assortment of books and magazines stacked in several piles on the floor. At one end of the room were two chairs, one with a painting on it: a seascape: somewhere in Cornwall – blue sky, brown cliffs, green grass on top slanting down to foam-tipped waves. It was on a piece of hardboard he'd given her – part of a panel off a bedroom door sawn up. He recognized the row of panel-pin holes along the bottom and the patch of canary yellow hard gloss showing through in a corner of the sea. On top of the cliffs, just visible through a thin wash of white, were the three houses he'd advised her to paint out.

He sorted through her paints, put what he wanted in a plastic carrier-bag together with some paint-smudged postcards of Gower scenes and went back downstairs.

His father was at the kitchen table sorting through some letters. He'd had the bill from Eynon's, he told Perkins: 'Two hundred and sixty three pounds fifty including V.A.T.' There was the breakdown if he wanted to see it. Perkins picked up the bill and glanced his eye down it: casket, robe, hire of cars, hearse – everything neatly itemized. His father handed him a plain, manila envelope: 'Then this came this morning,' he said. 'From the Town Hall. They've got a Book of Remembrance up in the Crem and you can pay so much to have an entry put in. I've circled the one I think I'll have.' Perkins emptied the envelope onto the table, It contained a pink and a green form and a two page brochure. The Book, it said, was beautifully bound in natural calf vellum and was composed of leaves of the finest sheepskin vellum, lettered by highly-skilled craftsmen. Kept in a protective case at the Crematorium, it would remain open each day at the appropriate page so that entries might be seen on each anniversary of the date of death. Opposite this general information was reproduced a facsimile page and a sample entry on this had been circled in blue biro:

Dawlings, Francis Marmaduke
1868. Love's last gift, remembrance. 1953.

'What do you think?' his father said. 'Do you think that's the best one?'

Perkins glanced down the list of other sample entries and nodded. 'I don't want anything too long,' his father said. 'It's £4.32 for two lines and then everything over that, of course, is more. But I think it's best to keep it simple.'

He took the brochure back and turned to the back page. You could have a Memorial Card as well, he said, or there was also a Miniature Book of Remembrance: '"*The Miniature Book has a full binding in vellum, gilt-edged with gold-blocked design, resembling the original Book of Remembrance. There is a title page and a four page centre on which, under the anniversary date is a handwritten copy of the original inscription as it appears in the Book.*" That's £7.56 – but I don't want to bother with that. Just the two lines is enough, I think.'

Perkins nodded and handed the envelope back. 'Yes, that's the best,' he said. 'The two-liner: not too short, not too long.'

7

Perkins sat on the settee looking out of the French windows at the rain-drenched lawns and the pink gravel drive where eight plastic 'boules' – four red, four blue – and two rackets and shuttlecock were randomly lying. Three towels and a bathing costume draped a hedge and beneath it a yellow and blue inflatable dinghy with two oars sticking out, lay stranded. It was mid afternoon on the second week in August somewhere in Northern Brittany. His wife was in the kitchen washing some smalls and the two kids were sitting down temporarily occupied filling in days one two and three of their holiday journals. They didn't have a lot to write about. Owain had devoted two pages plus an illustration to an abandoned life raft that had been hauled aboard on the crossing from Plymouth, and Mathew had written a graphic description of an incident in St. Malo the previous day, when Perkins had locked his keys in the car. It was going to be a long holiday. Perkins surreptitiously poured himself another glass of cheap red wine and knocked it back at a gulp. 'How many's that you've had now?' Owain said, without looking up.

'None of your business,' Perkins said.

'I'll tell Mummy.'

'You do and I'll – '

'Give me five francs for a comic then.'

'No chance – you've spent enough already.'

'I'm going to tell Mummy – '

Perkins jumped up just as his wife came in from the kitchen, wiping her hands in her apron. 'Tell Mummy what?' she said.

Owain smirked across at his father: 'Daddy's just drunk a whole bottle of wine,' he said.

She took a tablecloth from a drawer and spread it on the table: 'Don't worry – I know how much he's had. He wants to end up an alcoholic – it's a family tradition. Ah, well – it's *his* liver.'

Perkins laughed: 'Don't be silly,' he said. 'You could drink gallons of this stuff and it wouldn't affect you. It's only 9% proof.'

She clattered some cutlery onto the table. 'We need bread,' she said. 'I don't mind when you get it as long as it's in the next ten minutes.' Perkins crossed the room, accidentally treading on Owain's foot as he did so. 'May as well go now, then,' he said.

Though it was still lightly drizzling, he decided to walk. It was about a mile and a half along a deserted main road to the nearest shops. He stopped at the telephone kiosk on the corner, went in, put two 20 centime pieces in the slot and dialled a number on the International system. After a buzz and a couple of clicks, he could hear a purring sound. It was a full half minute before the phone was picked up at the other end:

'Hello – Dad?'

'Alvin?'

'Yes.'

'Where are you?'

'France, of course.'

'Everything all right? What's the weather like?'

'Drizzle.'

'It's sunny here – '

'What're you doing?'

'I've just come down off your roof. I've been fixing that aerial for you. You should have a good picture now.'

'Thanks.'

'…Westward isn't too good, though. You'd have to turn it a bit to get that perfect – but then you'd lose out on the others.'

'Leave it then.'

'If I turned it just a bit you'd get all the channels but none of them perfect – '

'Leave it as it is then – you'll never get it perfect. Any letters for me?'

'Nothing much: a couple of bills, a few circulars – oh! and a letter from the Times Literary Magazine – '

'The Times Lit Sup!' Perkins exclaimed. 'What does it say!'

'Hang on a minute – I'll just go and get it – 'There was a long pause…A tall man in sandalled feet with a raincoat over his head, appeared outside the box. ' – Here it is,' his father said after a bit. The pips started to go. Perkins dug in his pocket and fumbled a few more coins into the slot. 'What does it *say*?' he said.

'Not a lot,' his father said. 'Not even *Dear Sir* – just *"Thank you for sending the enclosed manuscript but we regret to say we are unable to use it on this occasion."* No signature or anything. There's some of your poems in with it. Do you want me to send them on to you?'

'No thanks. It doesn't matter.'

'…Are you having a good time?'

'Great.'

'How's Liz and the kids?'

'Fine.'

'The garden's in a bad way with you.'

'I know. I haven't had time – '

'It's looking so bad because it's in full growth this time of year.'
'I know. I'll have to do it when I get back.'
'I think I'll paint that gate of yours, too, now the weather's fine.'
'It's alright, Dad – *I'll* do it.'
'It needs a good scraping down and a primer of red lead first – '
'Its okay – *I'll* do it.'
'Take things a bit at a time, that's the best.
'Don't worry – I will. How's the dog?'
'Alright – she's just around my legs now.'
'Put her on.'
'Okay. Hang on…she's by the phone now – '
'Gypsy! Gypsy! *Good girl*, Gypsy!'
'She's wagging her tail.'
'Hello, Gypsy…good girl, Gypsy – *fetch!* **Fetch!**'
'How's the car going?'
'Like a bomb. I've only had one flat so far and a blown gasket.'
'*When!*'
'Only joking – '
'It's no joking matter, my boy. Don't forget you've got a wife and two kids to think about. You mind how you go. There's some mad buggers driving about out there.'

'I will. How are you, anyway? What've you been doing with yourself?'

'Your aerial for one thing. Watching the cricket. A bit of gardening – and now your gate.'

'Listen, Dad, there's a bloke waiting outside. Leave the gate to *me*. I better hang up – '

'Alright, but you may as well wait for the pips – ' The pips started to go. 'So-long now then mind how you go in that car watch those kids don't get sunstroke and look after – ' His voice cut out and a high-pitched hum replaced it. Perkins put the receiver down and on his way out said *'Pardonnez-moi, monsieur,'* to the man with the raincoat over his head.

8

Perkins and his family pulled up outside the house at two in the afternoon after five hours on the road. 'What's happened to the gate?' his wife said. 'It's *red!*'

Perkins switched off the ignition: 'Oh, I forgot to tell you,' he said. 'My father said he might paint the gate while we were away.'

'It looks as though he *has*. When did he say that – I didn't hear him?'

'In France,' Perkins said. 'I gave him a ring one day.'

'You didn't tell me,' she said.

'I forgot.'

'Well, I don't *want* it red. It looks terrible. It doesn't go with the rest of the house.'

'That's not the final coat,' Perkins said. 'That's just a primer.'

'I don't care what it is. I either want it off or I want it painted over – quickly.'

'OK, I'll see to it.' Perkins got out of the car and began organizing the unloading. They went indoors and were pulled up short by a strong smell of cat shit and a note pinned to the bannister:

> *Alvin and Liz,*
>   *Hope you had a good*
> *time and were not too sea-sick. Dog*
> *with me. Cat outside – I think… Some*
> *fish fingers in the fridge and some*
> *milk – enough for a cup of tea. You can*
> *bring my present down later. HA HA.*
>   *Love Cliff*
> *P.S. I painted the gate red. It's just*
> *a primer!*

'There you are,' Perkins said, handing the note to his wife, 'I told you it wasn't the final colour.'

The front door was ajar when he went down to his father's that evening. He called out and went through into the kitchen where his father was sitting at the table repairing an electric razor. He looked sunburnt and fit. 'Everything all right?' he said. 'I thought you might not sail. The forecast was terrible.'

'Gale Force nine,' Perkins said. 'A lot of yachts went down off Fastnet.'

'I know. It's been on the News. They're still looking for survivors.'

Perkins placed a bottle of Cointreau on the table.

'You shouldn't have bothered,' his father said. 'I was only kidding about the present. Do you want a drop?'

'Better not. I'm driving.'

'Have a drop of my ginger beer then – ' He got up and went into the kitchenette. 'Did you see the gate?' he called out.

'Yes.'

'What did you think of it?'

'Alright.'

'But that's only the first coat.' He came back in with two cups and handed one to Perkins. 'I'll do the second coat,' Perkins said.

'I'll do it,' his father insisted. 'I've got plenty of time now.'

They strolled up the garden with their drinks. The lawns were like billiard tables. A new crop of beans stood in regimental rows next to rows of spuds and onions and cabbages.

'The apples look good this year,' Perkins said.

'They haven't come fully yet,' his father said. 'Around early September they'll be at their best. I'll bring you some up.'

Perkins picked one and bit into its shiny sourness: 'You're right,' he said, tossing it away. 'They need at least a couple of weeks.'

They wandered round behind the shed where a huge bonfire was smouldering under a mound of clods and garden waste, a thin skein of smoke drifting lazily up from it. 'That's been going for weeks now,' his father said, 'ever since you've been away – ' He picked up a garden fork and raised the underneath of the pyre: there was an instantaneous crackle and rush of air as sparks billowed up in a thick white plume. He held the fork at arms length as the flames took hold then dropped it abruptly as the whole of one side went up volcano-like. Smoke engulfed him. He cursed and swore, screwing his fists up to his eyes. Perkins stood back momentarily mesmerized as the flames leapt higher and higher, licking the lower leaves of next door's horse-chestnut, floundering up and filling its branches...

9

Perkins and his wife liked to think they had open minds on the subject of the Supernatural but Mrs Tyke, their near-neighbour, was really hooked on it – a spiritual main-liner, if ever there was one. She'd been going to one or other of the two Spiritualist Churches in Town three or four times a week for years – ever since her first husband left her with two kids, one on the way and an impossible mortgage to pay off. 'It gives you ope,' she was fond of saying.

All the little Tykes were converts too, and often accompanied her. They were always 'seein things' as their mother put it, and wandered around with mysterious, faraway looks on their pale-white faces.

'Ere's proof then,' Mrs Tyke had said out of the blue one morning almost a year after the funeral, as Perkins and his wife were getting into their car. It was the usual sort of thing. The night before, Mrs Tooze the Psychic Artist from Clydach had seen Mrs Tyke sitting at a sick bed and asked if there was anyone ill in the family. No – not that Mrs Tyke knew of. But then – *guess what!* – when she got home there was a note on the mat saying her little nephew was down with scarlet fever and would she please call in. *'There's* proof for you!'

'Incredible,' Perkins had said and then, as he drove off, surprised his wife by asking if she'd like to go to the next meeting. His motives were purely literary he quickly added. He was interested as much in people's motives for wanting proof as in the proof itself – besides which, there was almost certain to be a story in it. His wife, who'd dabbled a bit in Ouija boards and had once been told, correctly, by an Irish gypsy that she was going to have her gall-bladder removed, readily agreed. Mrs Tyke was 'thrilled to bits' when they bumped into her again later the same day. She'd had a feeling they were going to go. The following Saturday would be the best time she said. That was when this Mrs Tooze was next reading. 'And I ope you'll ave somethin. She doan always get roun to everyone – but even if she doan is somewhere to go an, after all, it don't cost nothin do it?'

Saturday came and at ten to seven on a bright, sunny evening, they picked up Mrs Tyke outside her house. She was all dolled up to the nines and as excited as if she were going to the Top Rank for Bingo. *'Guess what!'* she said as she got into the car. *'Ere's* proof for you,' and she went on to tell them in vivid detail – all the way from the house to the Church – about Mr Connors her neighbour who'd recently died. 'E was always laughin at me and sayin "You'll be seein fairies next!" Well, I used to put the odd bet on for im down at the Bookies an last night at the Hoo Street Church there was a message for me from someone beginnin with C sayin "Aymarket, 3 o' clock." What d'you think of that? *There's* proof for you!'

The Church was in a back street behind Jake's Ice-cream Parlour and directly above a Second-hand Junk shop. A crumbling, red-bricked building with a paint-peeled wooden sign above the door, you'd easily miss it unless you were looking for it. They climbed the steep wooden stairway and were greeted at the top by a friendly, slightly effeminate young man wearing a woollen anorak, chords and sneakers: 'Thursday night's Medium,' Mrs Tyke explained.

The room was large and square and furnished like a Sunday School. Five rows of wooden chairs on one side, faced a dais on the other, on which stood a draped lectern, dominated by a large wooden cross on the wall behind. There was a small altar-like affair in front of this on which were a vase of flowers, another smaller cross, a Family Bible, a cardboard collection-box decorated with stuck-on wallpaper and, inexplicably, a pink fluffy toy elephant. An assortment of odd carpet pieces covered the floor and the walls were decorated with various biblical texts and pictures. One of these, Perkins recognized as being ex-Woolworth's: an early holographic depiction of The Last Supper. The room was day-lit and somewhere out of sight behind a heavy curtain next to the altar, Perry Como was singing Ave Maria.

There were only about eight other places already taken – mostly by elderly or middle-aged women – and they sat down in a near empty row, Perkins on the end next to his wife. Mrs Tyke leaned across: 'They sells raffle tickets in a minute,' she whispered. 'Thas the only trouble with comin early – but you don't ave to buy one if you don't want.' What were they raffling, his wife wanted to know.

'Is usually a box of chocolates – or a tin of somethin.'

'Ectoplasm,' Perkins suggested out of the corner of his mouth. The quip was lost on Mrs Tyke. 'On a Wednesday they aves an Ealin Service,' she explained, 'an next week they got a Flower Service – thas really good. You brings along a flower – any flower what you've picked youself an ands it in in a marked envelope. No-one else mus touch it – so the flower's only got your aura on it. Is what they calls psychometry. You wanna come to that. Everyone gets a readin that night – '

There were about eighteen people scattered around the room and those who wanted to, had already bought a raffle ticket from the cheery young Medium who had manned the door. Perry Como suddenly cut out, all talking stopped and there was now a fat, pasty-faced woman wearing glasses sitting just head and shoulders visible behind the lectern. She had tightly curled black hair that stood out starkly against her white scalp and piggy blue eyes. An elderly gentleman who looked like the late actor who'd played the late Jack Walker from Coronation Street – and may well have *been* him for all Perkins knew – stood up beside her and welcomed everyone to the meeting. 'Bless you! Bless you, friend!' called the young Medium from the wings.

'Well, it's fine out,' Jack Walker said, looking towards the window, 'but I know it will be fine *inside,* too, before very long.' He was simultaneously blessed from several quarters and, after giving a few brief announcements, said that before they began, Mrs Tooze would like to say a word. He sat down and Mrs Tooze sea-sawed up, not much taller now than when she'd been sitting. For such a big woman, she had a surprisingly small voice – refined and strangely old-fashioned – like a presenter on a 50's Children's Hour programme. She began with a short prayer for world peace and the protection of the animal kingdom and concluded with a proverb that most of those present seemed to already know, since they joined in reciting it: 'Always remember,' she said, 'that yesterday is tomorrow's today, today is tomorrow's yesterday and tomorrow is yesterday's today.'

Perkins was still trying to work that one out when the first hymn struck up – sung unaccompanied from green, typewritten song sheets. This was closely followed by a second hymn, during which a 'free-will donation' was taken. Then Mrs Tooze stood up again. She looked round the meagre congregation for a moment and pointed across the room at one of two elderly women sitting together. A beat-up fur stole draped around the woman's shoulders framed a thin, haggard face with sickly yellow skin and large, vacant eyes.

'Can I take the little one over there?' Mrs Tooze began.

The woman hardly stirred. 'Thank you, friend,' she said in a tired croak.

'Louder, please. I must hear the voice.'

'*Thank you*, friend!'

Mrs Tooze's eyes closed. She held a hand momentarily to her forehead, frowning: 'There is an Emily with me,' she said. 'Does that mean anything to you?'

'Yes.'

'This Emily passed into the spirit world before her time...she didn't want to go...'

'Yes.'

'...her passing was very long-drawn out and very painful but she is telling me now that she understands, that you're not to worry and that she is by your side all the time...'

'Thank you, friend.'

'...There is also a member of the police force here in spirit. Can you accept him?'

A moment's pause, then: 'Yes.'

'...and a white dog that passed on...'

'Yes – my mother's.'

Mrs Tooze frowned again: there were also a Mother Mary, a deceased postman, a certain Mr Clement, a Zulu and an Ancient Egyptian belly-dancer (who was the woman's spirit guide) present. The second of these, whom the woman had formerly known, had various cryptic messages for her which she received matter-of-factly with no outward show of emotion.

'You have not been well lately have you, dear?' Mrs Tooze continued.

'No, I haven't'

'You've been doing too much. Do you know that song *'Hold That Tiger'*? Well, they're all singing it here and I have to tell you that you *will* get better, but that you have to take things a lot easier.'

'I will friend.'

'I have to give you half a loaf: you'll never be rich but you'll never be poor. And I also have to say to you: "Time is a great healer." Can you understand that?'

The woman shook her head: 'No, friend, but I'll hold it.'

'Yes. Will you take that home with you, please. Thank you and God bless you, little one.'

More readings followed and each time Mrs Tooze glanced round the room for her next subject, Perkins looked away, not wanting to catch her eye. Some of the insights seemed spot-on. Did the old lady in the third row know a Delilah? The woman's eyes lit up and without a moment's hesitation: 'Yes, friend!' she said. 'Delilah Smith – from my school days.' Did a photograph of soldiers in uniform mean anything to the gentleman at the back? 'Yes!' he beamed, 'I was looking at it only this morning.' What did the word *'cigar'* mean to the genial Medium? He smiled ruefully: 'I smoked one for the first time the day before yesterday. I couldn't stand it so I threw it away.' Other readings seemed way off beam, either in part or in their entirety: Would the little old lady in the corner accept a window-cleaner? She would but she didn't know who he was. Well, would she accept him please, because he was standing there with a bucket of water and a rag. Did the name *"Molly"* have any significance for the bald-headed gentleman behind Perkins?

A definite 'No.'

Or a parrot?

'No.'

Or Walter Pidgeon?

'No.'

Or a laburnum tree?

'No.'

Or a sailor called Frank?

'Can't think who that can be – but I'll take it home with me.'

She thanked the man and blessed him anyway, bestowing on him *'The Gift of the Golden Ear'* – and could she leave him with a wet Fish Shop and an Indian guide called Dakota?

Mrs Tooze opened her eyes and Perkins looked quickly away. '…And now our friend over there – ' he heard her say. His wife dug him sharply in the ribs and he looked up to see the clairvoyant's finger pointing directly at him: 'Thank you,' he mumbled.

'A little louder – '

'Thank you!'

Her eyes were once more closed, forehead creased in concentration: '…I have the name *'McCarthy'*. Does that mean anything to you?' Perkins said that it didn't but that he'd take it home with him. The significance of the song *'Release Me'*, *'Rome wasn't built in a day'* and *'Post Office'* also escaped him, though he lied about the last, to break the run of negative responses. He'd recently smelt smoke around the house, hadn't he – as though someone had been smoking? No, he had to admit he hadn't.

'…Have you been feeling dejected lately – rather depressed? Well, you are coming out of that now. I have to tell you that things are going to change for the better. You are going to be financially better off. Where once you had one penny, you will now have two.' Perkins thanked her. She paused, frowning hard…'There is a lady here who was married twice and who recently passed into the spirit world. She had three sons. One by her first marriage, two by her second. Does that mean anything?'

'Yes.'

She paused again, one hand to her ear, smiling: 'Oh dear, there are so many, so very many people here now...they're all laughing and dancing for joy because they weren't expecting you and they're so glad that you've come...and now this lady is roaring with laughter...It's so funny she says...*Collis Browne's Mixture* – does that mean anything? She says it is the cure for all ills and she is laughing so much because she used to shovel it down the whole family when they were ill...and I have to tell you – she wants me to tell you – she is sending you *The Blue Bird of Happiness* on a silver plate...'

Perkins thanked her again but she wasn't finished yet. Now she had the name *'Kate'* – could he understand the name *'Kate'*?...No, he couldn't...nor the significance of the expression *'up up and away'*. She took a swig of water from a green glass goblet and changed tack bathetically: there were various odd jobs around the house he'd been putting off doing and now was the time to get them done. There was no time like the present. He had an Arab guide and he was going to London – 'or *somewhere over the water*.' She opened her eyes: 'You are a psychic powerhouse, my friend,' she concluded, 'and you have the gift of clairvoyance and healing. Thank you and God bless.'

They came out into bright evening sunlight. 'There you are – what did I tell you!' Mrs Tyke said, bubbling over as they got into the car: 'You ad somethin after all – first time, too. I'm glad o that – it gives you encouragement. See ow your luck as changed: you're goin to come into money, you're goin to London, you got an Arab guide an what are you – a psychic powerouse with the gift of clairvoyance an ealin!'

'Is that good?' Perkins said.

'Course it is – very good. All I got is 'The Gift of the Velvet Touch' an you can't do a lot with that.'

They started for home. 'Who d'you know called Kate?' his wife asked. Perkins didn't know anyone. Could be his Grandmother – she was Catherine but she may have been called Kate.

'Collis Browne's Mixture? Did your mother ever give you that?'

'Not as far as I know.'

'McCarthy?'

'Means nothing to me.'

Mrs Tyke leaned forward from the back seat: 'What about the Blue Bird of Appiness then,' she said. 'I never eard of that one before, but that sounds *very* lucky.'

It was 10p.m. Perkins wrote for an hour but didn't really have his mind on it. He put the pen down and sat, arms folded, staring out of the window, trying to let his mind go blank. After a while, out of the grey ether, unbeckoned and for no particular reason, a face appeared.

He went upstairs on the pretext of getting a book. His wife was in bed reading and hardly noticed his entrance. He knelt down by the bookcase and ran a finger along the rows. 'I think I know who McCarthy is,' he said.

She didn't hear him properly first time. 'The meeting this evening – I think I know who McCarthy could be,' he said. 'Desmond McCarthy – a kid in the Infants School I used to know.'

She looked at him, puzzled. He fingered the bookcase, his back half-turned to her, feeling slightly foolish now but obliged to go on: 'Funny thing – I'd forgotten all about him until tonight. He was as poor as a church mouse. Used to come to school in rags. I remember telling my mother about him and she told me to bring him home to tea one day. I'm sure *his* name was McCarthy.'

There was a momentary silence. 'Is he dead?' she said.

Perkins pulled out a book and flicked open the pages: 'How would I know. I haven't seen him for thirty years.'

She looked thoughtful: 'Yes,' she said. 'And that was funny, too – her mentioning about the Post Office.'

'What about it?'

'You know – my *father*' – she clapped shut her book – 'For Christ's sake, Alvin: he worked there all his life!'

Perkins shrugged and got up. 'I suppose it was funny,' he said, 'but it's a bit thin, isn't it? There's tens of thousands of people work in the Post Office.'

He went out quickly without waiting for a response, but in less than a minute came barging back in again: *'Kate Roberts!'* he said. His wife looked up, startled. 'Kate Roberts!' he said. 'Don't you remember – a few weeks ago when Gerry called. He saw that photo I'd taken of my mother – the one in my room – and thought it was Kate Roberts the writer – '

His wife yawned and rolled over on her side. 'Come and massage my back,' she said. 'I've been dying to feel those healing rays of yours all night. Or better still – let Ahmed do it.'

'Ahmed?'

'Your Arab Guide.' She laughed into the pillow: 'Mrs Tyke's got an Egyptian Princess – perhaps if you asked her nicely, she'd do a swop.'

Perkins sat on the edge of the bed and reached under the sheets. 'That bit was a load of bullshit,' he said, slowly beginning to rub. 'They always say an Arab or an Egyptian – or a North American Indian. It's so obvious. It was *all* so obvious really. Did you notice the way she was making asides all the time, as though there was someone else with her? That looked really phoney. And I *loved* the way she interrupted one reading to call on *'The Healer'* to heal her sore throat – that was a real stroke of inspiration – ' He chuckled and rubbed more vigorously.

His wife groaned under his touch. 'I don't know why you're laughing, though, Alvin,' she said. 'You know you believe in it, really. You're awfully superstitious. You're scared of ghosts and the dark, aren't you? So, deep down, you must believe in this, too.'

Perkins withdrew his hand: *'Who's* superstitious!' he said. 'Don't make me laugh – '

'You're one of the most superstitious people I know. Always have been.'

'Over some things, maybe,' he conceded, 'but – *this!*'

His wife yawned again and pulled the sheet up half way over her head. 'Well, I'm still keeping an open mind,' she said. 'I don't care what you say: that bit about the Post Office was very strange. Why should she pick on that? And why should she say the woman was married twice and had three sons and had only recently passed over? How could she possibly have known about your half-brother? It all fits. It's gotto be Alma – and she must be sending you The Blue Bird of Happiness.'

Downstairs again, Perkins went straight to his bookcase and thumbed through some back numbers of The Cambrian Review. After some searching he found the portrait head he was looking for and held it up to the one he'd taken of his mother. There was no doubt about it: there was a striking resemblance: hair, eyes, age, expression – even the lighting was similar. If he half-closed his eyes, it could almost *be* his mother. He ran back upstairs to show his wife but the light was out and she was already snoring faintly in the darkness. He came back down, propped the magazine up on the mantelpiece next to the picture of his mother and sat down at his desk. He looked at both photographs for a long time, comparing. After a while, it came into his mind that the Kate Roberts one also bore a striking resemblance to his wife's grandmother – and even Nelly Morgan, his mother's old friend – looked more like them, in fact. Both portraits, the more he looked, could almost be composites – identikit images for Old Age anywhere and everywhere, for innumerable Kates and Almas living or dead.

It was long past midnight and he had to be up early in the morning. Before he called it a day, he opened the top drawer of his desk and from a crumpled bag took the two halves of a broken pair of women's bi-focal glasses. He turned them over in his hands for a moment then held them up to his eyes and looked out to sea. Everything was a blur. A lightship blinked and a car signalled somewhere down in the amber depths of the Town. He put the two halves carefully back in the bag and slid the drawer shut.

To Liu and All Mankind

'I've been given the name of a Chinese political prisoner,' she said. 'He's a Father.'

'How many children's he got?' Perkins said, sipping at his fourth or fifth glass of home-made Hock.

'Don't be smart,' she said. 'He's a priest and he's in prison. I don't know what for or for how long. But I'm going to send him a Christmas card.' She reached in her handbag: 'Which of these two d'you think he'd like: this one or this one – ' She held up two cards: one an Old Master Nativity, the other a frivolous cartoon-y snow scene.

'I don't know,' Perkins said. 'I just don't know.'

'D'you think he'd like the religious one or the cartoon one? I think I'll send him both. What shall I put in the letter? I can't very well wish him a happy Christmas. What shall I put?'

Perkins tried to think but there was something on TV he wanted to watch: a French film – a love story. She put the cards down and looked, too: two lovers in bed naked by a blazing log fire. The girl with long blonde hair, the man with a Brillo-pad chest. 'I bet you any money she gets up,' Perkins said. 'She's going to get up and put a log on the fire – ' The girl threw back the sheet, revealing her breasts, but didn't get up. The man got up.

'What shall I put?' she said, picking up a card.

'Bet you he'll poke the fire,' Perkins said. 'They love a bit of symbolism, the French – ' The man left the fire alone and, instead, fixed a drink for himself and the blonde.

'What shall I *put*?' she persisted.

'What's his name?' Perkins said.

'Liu.'

'"Dear Liu,"' Perkins dictated, eyes still glued to the set, '"Chin up. It could be worse. Going anywhere for Christmas?"'

'Very funny,' she said. 'I've got to put something. He's a Roman Catholic. What would be best?'

The film was rapidly hotting up – the drinks fast hitting the spot.

'I know – I'll put "our thoughts are with you",' she said. He nodded sagely and emptied his glass, still transfixed.

'Can I put two cards in one envelope, I wonder? Shall I seal it? Can you imagine: they're so short of pictures out there, the warders'll probably keep them. Maybe they'll give him the cartoon one but they won't give him the religious one. Probably throw that in the bin. Probably killed him by now anyway – ' She glanced up, catching sight of his empty glass. 'You're a right lush, d'you know that? How many's that you've had now? You can't even wait for the stuff to settle – '

Owain came in before Perkins could reply and sat on the floor, three feet from the grappling lovers. 'Owain,' she said, 'if you were a Father – a priest – in a Chinese prison over Christmas, what would you like someone to write to you? I can't get any sense out of Daddy. Which of these two cards would you like to get?'

Owain didn't look round. He was going through that difficult period between early puberty and late manhood. 'If I was getting beaten shit out of by Chinese guards,' he said, 'I wouldn't give a toss which card I got. Send him a porno one. He's away from women. I'll cut up one of my nack mags if you like – '

'Thank you all very much for your concern,' she said. 'The *dog's* going to have a better time than this bloke and that's all you can say. Well, I'm going to send him both cards and I'm going to put "our thoughts are with you" – '

Perkins revitalized: 'My thoughts are with him,' he said, 'but there's not a lot you can do for the poor bastard. He probably doesn't even understand English. "Our thoughts are with you" is as good as anything – but there's no point in dwelling on it. If he gets it, he gets it; if it cheers him up, it cheers him up. That's all there is to it. That's all you can do.'

'You're a heartless bugger,' she said. 'You don't really care whether he gets a card or not.'

'Send it,' Perkins said. 'Put three cards in if you like. I think it's a brilliant idea. Pity more people don't do it – ' His eyes were back on the screen now and the writhing tangle of flesh. The sound of sighs and the frenzied crackling of logs filled the room. *"To Liu,"* she wrote in a large, clear hand, *"All our thoughts are with you"*…

After the Deluge

All night long, rain rattling above their heads on roof and windowpane, on their dreams and their dreamlessness and in the morning: silence and a strange, parched stillness. He lay studying the small rectangle of shadows in the portable TV: the mirror with grey-rosed wallpaper in, grey shelves, grey books; the shrunken bed with him and her in it, grey and foetal, ten thousand fathoms deep...Through the gap in the blinds, treetops waved outside, signalling in: face-making leaves and branches with sky holes in and empty sockets of eyes: live leaves next to the curtains' still ones – a moving mass of chlorophyll and light and photosynthesis.

The periscope hands of the Civic Centre clock tower had stopped. The tide was hill-high, the rows of rooftops, stepping stones leading down to and under it...

Small, infinitesimal sounds returned: the breeze outside and the sound of her snore and something that wasn't there before: a slow, rhythmic *pat pat pat*...He tried to home in on it, at first thinking it might be the drainpipe outside or the guttering. Then there were two sounds: a pit and a pat in unison. Something struck the carpet. He looked up. Towards the foot of the bed and over the bookcase were two bulges in the ceiling paper, a single drop of water welled at the bottom of each. He lay a moment, mesmerized, watching first one drop fall then the other, first one drop then the other... Then he galvanized into action, rolled out of bed, rushed downstairs and got two saucepans. Only a few old paperbacks had got wet, he was relieved to find when he returned, and the carpet was a bit squelchy, but other than that –. He aligned the saucepans directly under the drips, removed the books, put an old towel down on the damp patch and got back into bed. The pitterpats clanked on cold steel. He lay awake, counting the seconds between clank and clank, unable to go back to sleep for the din. His wife had begun to stir – a small hammer tap-tapping on the cast-iron womb of her dream. He went back downstairs and got a carving knife and a plastic bowl from the kitchen sink. Balancing precariously on the edge of the bed, he held the bowl under one of the bulges and jabbed with the blade. Nothing happened. He jabbed again and again creating three additional slow drips but no decrease in the bulge. Steadying himself and standing almost on tiptoe, he made a careful incision along the join of two runs of paper. The bulge burst open and emptied in one go, throwing him momentarily off balance. The bed springs twanged as he jumped down clutching the half-filled bowl to his chest. He emptied it in the bathroom, climbed back up on the bed and performed the same operation on the other bulge. His wife rolled over, opened her eyes and blinked in terror at the strange apparition silhouetted at the end of the bed, a knife in one hand and a bowl in the other. 'It's all right,' he said, quickly. 'We've sprung a leak – but I've fixed it now.'

Her eyes focused first on him, then on the two slits above his head. 'Oh my God,' she said, sitting bolt upright, 'what have you done to my ceiling!'

He took a step forward, lost his balance and jumped down, slopping water over his vest. 'Why?' she said, before he could say anything. 'Why did you do it?'

'It would have come through, anyway,' he explained. 'The weight of all that water. It was better to speed it along a bit – '

She was almost crying, as though it was she who'd been stabbed: 'It looks terrible. The whole lot'll have to be re-papered – '

'No it won't,' he said. 'Once it dries out, I'll glue that back easily. A tube of Copydex and some white emulsion and you won't know the difference – '

She flopped back exasperated onto the pillow. 'I've heard that one before,' she said. 'The whole house falling apart at the seams and you do a thing like that. It's getting to look like a slum as it is. We'll never be able to sell – '

She *was* crying now: tears flooded from her from a reservoir of resentment at the one-thousand-and-one jobs he'd botched or left undone over the years. She wanted the whole ceiling re-papered just as it was or as near as possible, since the paper was genuine Victorian and virtually irreplaceable. And she didn't want it done next week or next year she wanted it done right away. It took him a long time to placate her. He promised the ceiling would be done that very afternoon, along with several other small jobs he'd always intended doing but, first of all, he was going to make her breakfast in bed. She dried her eyes with the edge of the sheet. He tried to put his arm around her but she shrugged it away and he beat a discreet retreat, taking the half-full bowl and the carving knife with him.

Downstairs, he made a cup of tea and two pieces of toast with marmalade, arranged them on a tray together with the morning paper and took them up to her. She was asleep: her back to him, the sheet drawn half-way over her head as though to block out the sight of the ceiling. He put the tray down and slipped quietly in beside her, scarcely daring to breathe. It was still only just gone seven on a bright July morning. He lay looking up. Prematurely delivered of the night's downpour, the two gashes looked like two gigantic vulvae. He closed his eyes but they wouldn't go away: they gaped over his sleeplessness – two caves, two suppurating wounds, still intermittently dripping...

Storm in a Teacup

...two dark moon shapes like segments from a chocolate orange, side by side and tip to tip, forming a white porcelain ovoid between them. Nothing else of particular note, so far as he could make out but these two perfectly formed shapes. Vaginal almost...He handed her the cup:

'Lots of tears,' she said, rotating the dregs. '...*and a smiling giant...a deep crevasse...with a boat...a little steamer gliding down a river – either a river or a narrow strait – somewhere in Norway...*'

'Am I on board the steamer?' Perkins said.

'I can't see *you* anywhere,' she said. 'There's just a steamer and it's on one side of a ravine or a fjord. It's too far away to see who's on board. You might be, you might not.'

'What about the giant?'

' – a mountain or a giant. In profile he looks like a Native American chieftain – very proud – feathers on his head and two fingers raised.'

'Two fingers raised? What does that signify?'

'Peace.'

'Peace? I thought it meant *"up yours"*.'

'It looks as though the steamer has set sail and look! Look at that in the bottom.'

'What is it!' he said, making a grab for the cup.

'More tears,' she said. 'There's still a lot more tears left in the bottom.'

He took the cup back off her, tilted it swiftly to his mouth and drained the last few drops. Then he turned the cup upside down in the saucer, as he'd seen her do, rotated it three times and handed it back to her.

'Carry on,' he said.

She looked at him in disgust 'You can't do that,' she said. 'Just because you don't like what it's telling you, you can't rearrange it. You've got to accept what's there.'

'I hadn't quite finished drinking,' he said. 'Carry on with the reading. It's getting interesting.'

'There's no point now,' she said.

'Okay,' he said, 'I'll pour some more in a fresh cup – ' He poured another cup of the, by now, lukewarm tea and drank it in one go. She took the cup off him and examined the tea leaves:

'...*a crinoline lady,*' she said, 'like the ones your mother used to paint...*and a big balloon with a basket at the bottom of it...and a letter – no two letters – and a man riding a horse...*'   She looked up suddenly and saw that he was writing it all down in a notebook. She slammed down the cup, spattering tears all over the table cloth. 'Oh God that's sickening!' she said.

'What is?' Perkins said, looking up from the notebook, thinking she'd spotted something really cataclysmic this time.

'*You,*' she said, 'writing all this down, making me the subject of another fucking story. D'you have to record everything I do and say? It's so intrusive.'

'It's just the reading I'm recording,' he said. 'For future reference.'

'I'm not an object to be pinned down and analysed,' she went on, 'I'm a human being. I don't want to be depersonalized in prose.'

'I'm not trying to depersonalize you,' he said. 'This isn't *for* a story – '

'Writers are all the bloody same,' she said, in full spate now. 'D'you know what they remind me of? Blood-sucking vampires, stealing the moment. They're like these thick-headed explorers who take photographs of primitive peoples who don't like being photographed because they believe the camera steals their souls. That's exactly what you're doing now. You're an outsider barging your way into some remote tribal village and snapping away willy nilly: stealing everyone's soul.'

And without another word, she got up, took his cup and hers, went over to the sink and plunged them both into a bowl of soapy water.

May 13th

After tea and an hour's kip on the settee, Perkins went for his usual run. It was cold and desolate on the Bay: the tide high and hardly a soul in sight. He did a slow outward lap against the wind and a fast return following almost exactly in his own footprints. A dog nearly took a chunk out of his leg by the Docks but its owner called it off and Perkins kept on going: up and through the dunes and along the sea-lashed steps to the County Hall, past the wind-cheatered fishermen and the lone watchers-of-waves in their land-locked cars. 1.16.18 from garden gate to garden gate: three minutes 20 outside his Personal Best thanks to the wind and the dog and a tough day at the Chalk Face.

There'd been a funny smell in the passageway all week: a stale, musty sort of smell – as of damp mummy-cloths left too long in a spin-drier. Perkins had ignored it at first – the vague, uneasy nuance wafting around his coming and going – but now, as he came in, tired and profusely sweating, his wife finally focused his attention on it: had he noticed the carpet was damp and stained a fungus-y sort of white in a corner by the front door? The rubber underlay was damp, too, and the lino underneath and there were little woodlice crawling around all over the place having a whale of a time. While he'd been out enjoying himself jogging, she'd been down on her hands and knees having a look. There were a couple of loose floorboards in the same vicinity – as he well knew – which could mean wet-rot or dry-rot or God-knows-what. Something would have to be done…

It was evening when he came down from his shower, the Tide receded from the County Hall steps; the wind already eroding the waffle tread of his shoeprints somewhere outside in the drizzling darkness.

The smell at the foot of the stairs was still depressingly poignant. He sprayed it liberally with Clean-Air then got down on his knees and, like a fatalistic surgeon, peeled back the carpet – first incision – then the underlay. There was dark brown lino tacked down underneath and beneath that another layer of patterned stuff from an earlier dynasty. He pulled both layers back revealing the bare floor boards. They looked bone-dry and perfectly sound. He tapped and poked them all over with a screwdriver. The Nine o' clock News was just starting in the other room and upstairs his younger son was playing an old Beatles' L.P.

He let the four layers of floor covering fall back into place and went and consulted the Reader's Digest Home Repair Manual. It was full of useful hints and diagrams but lacking the necessary tools he returned with the screwdriver and made do with that, easing it into the crack between a long and a short plank and gently levering down. The wood cracked and strained under the pressure but gradually the floor brads began to give and the short board rose...A faint draught of cool air wafted up at him as it came away. He peered inside the gap. Eighteen inches down was a gloomy waste of rubble and dust, primordial cobwebs; no sign of fungus or damp, no sign of anything – except there, beneath a gap in the skirting board: a tiny green plastic shell from a long-obsolete field-gun, lying stranded like a solitary space-probe on the surface of Mars.

The combined weight of carpet and under-lays prevented the longer plank from coming away completely so he had to roll up the carpet and force back the lino even further from the wall. It was then that he noticed the corner of a piece of newspaper sticking out and a fragment of newsprint – a column heading. He had to twist his head to read it: 'LORD MILNER DEAD', it said. 'GREAT STATESMAN YIELDS TO SLEEPY SICKNESS. VISCOUNTY BECOMES EXTINCT'. He tugged at the lino now, ripping it in his new-found eagerness until another page and more columns revealed themselves: 'CABINET SECOND THOUGHTS ON THE BUDGET. CHURCHILL PLANS TO BE WHITTLED DOWN'...'DEATHCHAIR SMOKE OF A MURDERER. WALK TO EXECUTION SMOKING A CIGAR'...He pulled harder, insinuating his hand, his whole arm, beneath the lino to loosen the pages from the hidden tacks that held them until they came away: two, three, four whole sheets: pages from a Daily Express and the South Wales Evening Echo for 1925: Wednesday May 13th. 5.30 Early Edition. For a moment the significance of the day and the month eluded him. The pages were stained and worn right through in places but still perfectly legible. *'Sing Sing, Thursday:… threefold execution of convicted killers Maurice and Joseph Diamond and John Farina…'* he read, *'…Farina showed remarkable stoicism. He carried a crucifix in one hand and a lighted cigar in the other. He took his last puff, smiled, flicked the ash from his cigar, kissed the crucifix, said "Goodbye all," and died…'*

His wife was doing the crossword puzzle when he went into her. He lowered the volume on the TV and stood in front of it, the paper concealed behind his back: 'Guess what I found,' he said. She looked up, immediately misinterpreting his tone of voice and expression: 'Oh my God – *what!*'

'Some old newspapers – under the lino. Guess what the date on them is.'

She gave up straightaway, relieved that he had found nothing terminal.

'Guess,' he insisted.

'1949.'

'No.'

'Earlier or later?'

'Earlier – much earlier.'

'1749? I really don't know. I'm in no mood for games.'

'1925!' he said, waving the papers in front of her. 'May 13th, 1925. Isn't it the 13th today?'

She checked from the paper in front of her and found that it was. He could hardly believe it: *'May 13th!* – a three hundred and sixty four to one chance – ' He handed her some of the pages and in a moment they began reading each other extracts:

'First boater spotted in the Mumbles – '
'Horse runs amok in Wind Street – '
'Swansea seaman drowned off Ushant – '
'Snow at Sketty – '
'Swans gain promotion – '
'7 piece dining room suite – £15 – '
'The New Chevrolet – Cheaper and Better at £155 – '

'Rudolph Valentino in the Castle and Harold Lloyd in the Albert Hall: *"for joy unalloyed see Harold Lloyd!"'*

They swapped pages and read to themselves. Perkins couldn't get over the coincidence of the date. 'Think of all the things that have happened while these have been lying down there,' he said: 'The Depression, Prohibition, World War Two – and think of all the people who must have walked over them – '

His wife thought he ought to contact the Echo the next morning to see if they'd be interested in doing a story. Who could have put them there, she wondered. It couldn't have been the Cranfields – they'd only come there just before the War; it must have been the old lady who was born there – the one who now lived near his father. What was her name? Miss Tweney – that was it. She'd have been in her early twenties round about then. Why didn't he give his father a ring to find out? Perkins handed her his sheets and went and telephoned his father, carefully sidestepping the hole on the way. Over the phone, he learned of a second, even stranger coincidence: Miss Tweney, who was in her mid-eighties, had died the same week and been buried the day before. He hurried back to tell his wife, almost falling into the hole in his haste…

Oblivious now of his original intention of finding the source of the damp, Perkins worked late into the night untacking and lifting the lino along the whole length of the passageway. He worked with a grim determination, sweat dripping from him for the second time that day, his hands filthy, his trousers crumpled and covered in dust. No more pages came to light. His wife had gone to bed by the time he'd finished his excavations and the passageway looked as though a small bulldozer had been driven down it. He sat on the bottom stair surveying the scene, conscious suddenly that the mysterious smell of damp had dissipated – almost as though in raising the floorboards it had somehow been exorcized.

Before he replaced the boards and screwed them down and rolled back the several strata of floor covering and tacked them into place, he propped up a loose joist with some pieces of stone, discovering in so doing that the underside of the joist was riddled with worm holes. He didn't investigate further for fear of what he might find but turned his attention to scratching out a message in the foundation dust: 'A.P. Loves L.P.,' he started to write but the letters were practically illegible. Instead, on an impulse, he put the South Wales Evening Echo for that evening – with his wife's unfinished crossword inside – in the hole, together with a slim collection of his unpublished poems, which he signed and dated.

By the time he'd finished, fed the cat and dog and locked all the doors, everything was once more as it had been – except that the floorboards no longer creaked so loudly and the mysterious smell had definitely gone. He went upstairs and washed his hands thoroughly before changing in the dark of the landing.

His wife was already asleep. He regretted leaving the poems almost as soon as he climbed in beside her, and lay thinking of all the thousand and one things it would have been more appropriate to have left. Shadow branches shimmered on the wallpaper. Through the gap in the curtains, the sea was a misty blue pinpricked with lights. He had no idea of the time. The whole house seemed to creak. He closed his eyes and imagined the ghost of a man downstairs – fifty, a hundred years from then – poised over the gaping wound in the floor, dipping his hand into the blackness beneath the rib-cage of joists, calling to the ghost of his wife in the other room...

Starters

Perkins arrived in 9.36 at 7.04.06 precisely on a Friday evening wearing shorts, polo neck sweater, toggle hat, white woollen gloves and trainers. There was a light on in the front room but no answer when he rang the bell. He looked through the letterbox and could just make out the hunched figure of his father, sitting in an armchair watching TV. He rang again and in a moment the door opened.

A warm waft of air hit him. He trotted past his father into the front room and straight to the coal fire, where he remained trotting with his back to it, studying his watch.

'On your own?' his father said, glancing out into the night.

'– Nine thirty six! Not bad, eh?' Perkins said. 'Another PB.'

'PB?'

'Personal Best – my fastest time to date.'

His father closed the front door, turned and lowered the volume on the TV. 'How far have you come?' he asked.

Perkins stopped trotting: 'Only from the house,' he said. 'A mile and a half. Won't stop long – I'm covered in sweat.'

'Sit down and relax,' his father said. 'I'm just watching Pick a Card. There's a young couple trying for the Jackpot. Looks as though they're going to win it, too.'

'Don't let me stop you watching,' Perkins said, making his way out into the kitchen. His father followed, half turning to watch the outcome of the TV Quiz game. 'D'you want a towel?' he asked. Perkins was already in the bathroom using one. He came out drying himself and his father handed him another towel and asked if he wanted a cup of tea. Perkins declined, strolling back into the front room where the young couple were already hugging each other in the front seats of a spanking new car – audience cheering, organ frenziedly playing, the Quiz Inquisitor just winding up the Show.

They sat down by the TV: his father in front of it, Perkins alongside it. 'Don't let me stop you watching,' Perkins said again. His father leaned forward and switched it off, sending a luminous white line shooting across the blankness. The room was suddenly silent as he settled back into his chair and slowly removed his glasses. 'Everything alright?' he asked. 'Liz? The Kids?'

'Fine,' Perkins said. 'I've been busy the last few nights otherwise I'd have come down. Parents' evening with Mathew on Tuesday and I've had to take him for coaching other nights. I ran eight miles on Wednesday while he was having his Biology lesson – from the West Cross Inn to the lights at Union Street and back: fifty-four thirty-five but the wind was against me on the turn – '

His father nodded: 'Nice to know he's taking an interest in his work – he'll go far. Are you doing any writing these days?'

'No. Too busy running. Haven't got the energy for anything else.' He stretched out his legs and lay back in the chair, looking up at the ceiling. His father nodded, thoughtfully, momentarily at a loss for something to say. There was another pair of glasses on the arm of his chair. He picked them up and put them on: 'What do these look like on me?' he said, 'They're an old pair of your mother's bi-focals. She used them for reading. I'm thinking of getting the lenses changed to suit me. Course, I know they're a woman's but I don't mind that. I'll only be using them indoors for reading.'

'They look okay,' Perkins said. 'Like a woman's but okay.'

'Your mother had different coloured tops to put over these, to match whatever she happened to be wearing at the time but, of course, I won't bother with those. You try them – '

Perkins put them on. His father was in sharp focus from head to neck but blurred the rest of the way down. He handed them back and his father handed him his other pair of national health ones. Perkins put them on. His father was fuzzy through one lens, in fairly sharp focus through the other. He handed them back, together with his own glasses. His father tried them on, looked around the room, shook his head and handed them back.

'Is that sweat there?' his father said, indicating the dark stain on Perkins' vest..

'Yes,' Perkins said, jumping up abruptly and balancing on one leg, like Eros, bending at the knee and watching the muscle flex.

His father watched him shift from one leg to the other and carry out the same routine. 'Heard anything about the London Marathon yet?' he said.

'No, it's too soon. Probably hear just before Christmas.'

'You're not overdoin this runnin business, are you? I read an article the other day. It was saying that in America they did a test on a hundred manic depressives. One group was given psychotherapy, another was given medicinal treatment and the third group was given jogging sessions – '

' – And the jogging group was cured?'

'Ninety-nine percent of them. The other one dropped dead. Mind you, I've always said that that's what your brother should have been made to do years ago. It used to depress me to go up to that mental hospital and see them all sitting around like zombies. If I'd had my way I'd have had them all rounded up for exercise whether they liked it or not. When I used to cycle I used to be fit as a fiddle. Never depressed. Never had time to be.'

'It's good for everything,' Perkins said, balancing on his first foot again: 'Rheumatism, arthritis. Look at Jack O'Brien – over sixty and still rated number fifty-seven in Wales.'

'Running's alright in moderation,' his father said, 'but did you see that programme on the other night: *Your Life in their Hands?* Young athlete with back trouble. They showed the whole operation from start to finish. I don't think you could have watched it. They opened his back right up and you could see where this disc had been squashed out of place. Blood everywhere – '

Perkins strolled over to the fireplace to examine the ancient, familiar bric-a-brac that lined a shelf: clothes brush in clog brought back from Holland; beer tankard from Germany; Kipling's framed 'If'; pottery model of four of the Seven Deadly Sins...There were coloured faery lights draped around the mirror. 'Your mother put those up,' his father said. 'I haven't taken them down since the Christmas before last.'

Perkins did three quick knee bends and touched his toes twice.

'How far are you going to run back?' his father asked.

'Not far,' Perkins said, opening the front door: 'down to the Wesleyan Chapel, Derwen Fawr, Bible College, Blackpill, Brynmill, St.

Helen's, round behind the Westbourne and back up Constitution Hill – say six miles.'

'That's too much. You'll be having a seizure, just like your mother. Two miles is quite enough – oh, I almost forgot,' he said, shuffling over to the sideboard, 'I saved these for you – ' He handed Perkins two old, sepia-faded newspaper cuttings from the sideboard. On one was a picture of a crowd of runners and on the other, two columns of print headed *'Entries Cease for the Big Road Race.'*

'What's this?' Perkins said.

'The Annual Mumbles to St. Helen's Road Race – 1933,' his father said. 'That's me – five or six rows back, arrowed.'

Perkins could just make out the grinning, tousled head of his father poking out from among the fifty or sixty other runners. Over 30,000 spectators were expected to line the route said the accompanying article; all the noted harriers of West Wales would be present but the winner was hotly tipped to be a rank outsider. At the bottom of the second column was a list of entrants. 'You never showed me this before,' Perkins said.

'It was the only one I ever entered,' his father said. 'I only went in for it because my mate Ivor Bevan persuaded me. I was just an apprentice at the time.'

His father's name was halfway down the list of starters: *C.J. Perkins, unattached, Sketty.*

'Mumbles to St. Helen's – that's about four and a half miles,' Perkins said.

'And twice round the rugby pitch to finish – five miles in all. I can still remember the name of the bloke who won it: Raddon. From Manselton. Jack O'Brien was well up in the finishers and Ivor Bevan was tenth or eleventh. He's dead now – been dead these many years.'

'What did you come?' Perkins said.

His father smiled: 'Guess.'

'Second?'

'No.'

'In the first 50?'

'No.'

'Sixtieth? Seventieth?'

The smile on his father's face broadened: 'I didn't finish,' he said. 'I got as far as the Mayals and hopped on a bus.'

Perkins turned over the cuttings, shaking his head in mock disgust. There was an advert for a Parker Duofold pen on the back of one: *'Music, sublime but fleeting, was made immortal by the Parker Pen in the hands of the great Maestro Giacomo Puccini. To a friend he wrote: "The Parker Pen is superlatively good."'*

'Did anyone see you getting on?' he said, re-folding the cuttings.

His father was still smiling: 'I didn't think so, until I got into work the next day. In the tea break a young feller – an apprentice like myself – said "Didn't I see you getting on a bus yesterday?" It took me aback but I didn't lose my cool. I looked him straight in the eye and said "Say that again and I'll punch you right on the nose!" Eastman his name was. I don't think I've seen him from that day to this. That's almost fifty years ago now. You can keep that if you like – '

Perkins opened the front door and stepped out into the night. 'Give it to me next time,' he said. 'It'll get all sweaty in my shorts.'

His father stood silhouetted in the doorway as Perkins trotted down the garden path and marked time for a moment by the gate. 'Two miles,' his father called after him, 'You mark my words, my boy: two miles is quite enough !'

'Don't hang about in this cold!' Perkins called back. 'You'll catch your death!'

His father stayed put. Perkins glanced at his watch and broke into a trot, waving back to the shadowy figure in the doorway as he went. It was precisely 7. 15. 35. With luck and a following wind for most of the way, he'd be home and dry by approximately 8. 05.

Power

It went away in the wake of a distant thunderstorm. Perkins was in the garden at the time, attempting to strim two seasons' growth of grass, when the high-pitched whine of his strimmer abruptly cut out and he was left holding a dead, impotent thing attached to a lifeless umbilical.

He went straight indoors to check the power point and then out the kitchen where his son was standing by the ironing board pressing a pair of jeans by the fading heat of an iron. He'd been listening to a cassette of the Beatles, he explained, when everything had gone off at once: washing machine, spin drier, iron, fridge-freezer, clock and cassette recorder. It must have been a power cut.

Perkins wasn't so sure. He checked the lights and the room sockets and immediately spotted that the iron and the cassette recorder were both plugged into the same adaptor. 'What have I told you about overloading power points!' he snapped. 'And what the hell are you ironing jeans for, anyway. Aren't they *supposed* to look creased?'

Mathew protested that he'd had the iron and the cassette recorder on together lots of times. If it had been the socket there'd have been a flash or a spark. 'It's *their* fault,' he insisted. 'The Electricity Board's!'

Perkins still wasn't convinced. He began searching for the fuse box: first in the airing cupboard, then under the stairs – a hopeless task made more hopeless by the knowledge that even if he found it he didn't have a fuse and even if he did he wouldn't know which fuse to replace or how to replace it. He kept looking anyway, reckoning that he had perhaps an hour or so before the ice started to melt in the fridge-freezer. After a bit, it dawned on him that if anybody ought to know where the fuse box was, his father would. He picked up the phone and started to dial but the line was dead. Mathew finished pressing his jeans with the luke-warm iron, put them on and went out.

Now Perkins was on his own. He couldn't ring out and he didn't know what time it was or when his wife would be back. Perhaps it was a power cut after all. He ran down the steps and onto the street in time to catch a neighbour just going in through his back gate. The neighbour didn't know anything about a power cut but when he went and checked, found that everything was off in his house as well. On his way home he'd noticed an electricity van at the far end of the street, so perhaps that was something to do with it. Perkins went back indoors, relieved of the responsibility for finding the fuse-box and comforted that the whole street, maybe the whole Town, was in the same boat. He made himself a bowl of cornflakes – his second meal of the day – and sat down in the gloom of the kitchen sorry, all of a sudden, that he'd jumped to conclusions and blamed his son.

It was like dusk in the kitchen without the lights on. There was no direct sunlight at either of the two small windows, both of which looked onto outside walls. The electric clock was silent and the Baxi Bermuda boiler and the strip lighting above the sink…He sat there dark and sullen as Neanderthal man before his empty cornflakes bowl, listening. Suddenly and without warning, exactly as it must have been when he was first conceived, it afterwards struck him, everything started up again – instantaneously, like magic: the lights came on, the spin drier, the washing machine, the iron, the boiler, the fridge-freezer, the clock and the Beatles – in mid-lyric, precisely where they'd left off. Like a game of statues. Everything that had previously had movement and breath, breathed and moved again ten times louder and faster. Exactly like being reborn: at the snap of a finger, in the blink of an eye: the whole house recharged – silence then sound; lassitude then life; absence then presence; melancholy then mania…

Days of the Comet

They were sitting in the car in Tescos car park, loaded with groceries, about to drive off. It was a late and light-polluted November evening but she paused for a moment to gaze up through the windscreen. 'Look at the moon,' she said, 'there's a kind of haze around it. And look at that single star just above it – that's Venus, isn't it: the brightest star in the sky – ? '

Perkins hadn't a clue. Although it was bitterly cold and draughty in the car, he suddenly felt very randy. He tried to put his arm around her but she shrugged it away. There'd been a Science programme on in the morning she said, which had featured an item on Halley's Comet and also a piece about recent advances in medical science. The good news was that Halley's Comet was due back any day now, and that there'd been a breakthrough in the study of DNA, which would mean that scientists could keep people alive forever. The bad news was that they probably wouldn't be able to see the Comet and the DNA breakthrough had come too late to be of any use to either of them. Perkins wasn't unduly worried. He tried to embrace her again but she shivered and leant away.

For some reason, he felt like singing on the way back, giving vent to his pent-up lust. As they accelerated out onto the dual carriageway, he boomed out the opening bars of the Hallelujah Chorus, substituting 'Halley's Comet' for 'Hallelujah.'

Once it had passed, the Comet wouldn't be round again until the year two thousand and something, she told him. Would they see it second time round, he asked, knowing full well that they wouldn't. 'No, but Owain and Mathew might,' she said. 'They say it coincides with the birth of someone great.'

'Someone great is born even when it's not passing,' he said.

'I know – but this would be someone exceptional.'

'Like Attila the Hun,' he said, 'or Hitler or Margaret Thatcher, I suppose – ' He sang a few more bars of The Halley's Comet Chorus then had a sudden brainwave: Why didn't *they* have another one?

There was still time. He could be the Chosen One. She didn't think so.

'You don't think he'd be the Chosen One?'

'I don't think I want another one.'

He put his foot down hard and burst into song again. She joined in despite herself and they drove on hopelessly harmonizing. *The King-dom of this world –* ' they sang, forgetting what came after – humming it. They'd once sung The Hallelujah Chorus together in a combined choirs Festival when they were young, in the same church at the same time but unknown to each other then and in different choirs. So here was history repeating itself – for the first time in forty years – the two of them singing The Hallelujah Chorus together: the momentous occasion, like Halley's Comet, come round again. Maybe in another forty years they'd be singing it together in an Old People's Home – unless the DNA people came up with something pretty spectacular.

When they got home he sat down and wrote her a love poem – a short one but the first for some fifteen years. He read it through to himself half a dozen times to make sure it wasn't too cringe-making, then wandered into the living room where she was watching Star Trek and, after a moment, said: 'I've written you a love poem.'

'Oh my God!' she said, without looking up, so that he wasn't sure whether she was reacting to him or the on-screen action. The Star Ship Enterprise seemed to be desperately trying to break through some sort of invisible force field. It was a good nanosecond or two before he asked if she wanted to read the poem.

'Alright,' she said, still without looking up, ' – as long as it's not too long. I want to watch this – '

He hesitated: 'No – I'd better not show it to you. It's a bit sentimental.'

'Come on – let's have a look.'

'No.'

'Oh well – bugger you!' she said and went back to watching Captain Kirk struggling to restore power to the Enterprise's crippled engines.

He hovered in the doorway: 'D'you really want to see it?' he said.

'Either show it to me or go away.'

'You'll laugh.'

'No I won't.'

'Well, okay.' He produced the poem from behind his back. She took it from him, read the first three lines and started laughing. He tried to snatch it back off her but she held it away and carried on reading.

'Well, what d'you think?' he said, when she finally handed it back.

'Very nice,' she said.

'*Nice?* Is that all?'

'Well. what d'you expect me to say? Superb? Brilliant? I don't really understand it.'

He took it back off her and stuffed it in his back pocket. 'There's nothing to understand,' he said. 'It's a love poem, for Chrissake! I knew I shouldn't have shown it to you. But you're right – it's crap.'

'I didn't say it was crap,' she said, 'but I've told you before: I'm no judge of poetry. You should show it to one of your literary cronies – someone who knows something about it. It seems like quite a good poem – as far as I can tell – ' He stood there waiting for her to elaborate but her eyes were once more glued to the screen and the embattled Enterprise which was now zooming across the Universe at Warp 8 or 9, hotly pursued by a fleet of Klingons.

He went back out without a word, sat down at his desk and for the next twenty minutes or so stared out through the window – at the sea with his dim reflection in it staring blankly back at him. He was still staring when she called out from the other room. He delayed going in to her until she'd called a second and third time. Star Trek had finished by now and she was sitting on the settee with a bowl of eggs on her lap. 'What's the matter now,' he snapped. 'I was just in the middle of something – '

She picked up an egg, turned it over in her hand and placed it on a cushion along with several others. 'It said on the News,' she said, 'that every time the Comet comes round, they find the shape of a comet on an egg.'

'Who does?' he said.

'Someone does. Someone somewhere.'

'On how many eggs?'

'Just one. Every seventy six years. They're looking out for another one now.'

'What do they do with the egg when they've found it? Boil it, hatch it or what?'

'I don't know. They didn't say. All I know is they're looking out for another one.'

'That's bullshit,' Perkins said. 'Superstitious bullshit handed down by cranks and crackpots over the centuries.'

'No it's not,' she said. 'They've actually found the shape of a comet on eggs in the past and there's a bloke in Gellinudd who reckons he's just found one. They interviewed him on here. Showed the actual egg. The experts have got to check it first but if it's genuine, he stands to win £5,000.'

'If you look long enough you'll see anything in anything,' Perkins said. 'I bet there've been thousands of comet shapes on eggs laid in other years as well. It's just that nobody was looking for them then. It's all a big publicity stunt by the Egg Marketing Board. There's probably thousands of housewives up and down the country sitting with bowls of eggs on their laps at this very moment, all looking for comets. People attribute everything to comets: invasions, wars, earthquakes – '

'Well, there's nothing on any of these so far,' she said, turning over another egg.

'Take them back and complain,' Perkins said. 'Say you want one with a comet on it.'

Just then, Mathew came in – red-nosed and slightly breathless – from Night Class. He didn't take off his overcoat or say hello but went straight to the Welsh dresser, took out a pair of binoculars from the bottom drawer and started back out again. 'What's up?' Perkins said.

'Halley's Comet,' Mathew said. 'I've just seen it.'

Perkins' wife abandoned the eggs and went and called Owain

down from upstairs. Together, the three of them followed Mathew out the front. He had the binoculars trained due south, in the direction of Ilfracombe: 'Over there,' he said. 'I saw it moving – ' They all looked due south but Perkins knew it was pointless. 'You know what he's looking at, don't you,' he laughed. 'One of the floodlights on St. Helen's!' They ignored him and kept on looking. It was already getting very cold standing out there.

'It's supposed to be somewhere in that direction,' she said. 'Near Taurus – '

'That's a load of bull,' Perkins said. 'You're looking south and it's due to appear in the north – and not until mid-December and even then they doubt whether anyone will see it – even with a pair of binoculars.'

His wife took the binoculars off Mathew and started looking due west, over the garden wall. 'There it is!' she said, pointing up through the almost bare branches of the sycamore. 'It's over there by the Plough – '

'And look – there's Mars!' Perkins mimicked. 'That red light over Kilvey Hill – or could that be the light on top of the television mast!'

'Did you know,' she said, swinging the binoculars abruptly due east towards number 74's pine-end, 'that comet dust was responsible for the extinction of the dinosaurs?'

'Or that Halley's Comet appears in the Bayeux tapestry or that Giotto painted it in one of his Nativities or that Mark Twain was born and died in years of the Comet,' Perkins added.

The two boys went indoors, shivering. Perkins edged closer to her so that their two breaths mingled, curling up and away into the night. 'It's nonsense,' she said, still focusing, 'to say you can't see it with binoculars: you're supposed to be able to see it with binoculars or the naked eye – '

Her moon-struck face, locked heavenwards, looked suddenly frail and vulnerable. Perkins couldn't help himself: 'With the naked eye or with the naked *breasts*,' he said, clasping her abruptly round the mid-riff. She struggled free and pushed him away, laughing and cursing at the same time, and hurried indoors leaving him holding the binoculars.

Foiled again, Perkins stayed put on the patio, focussing the binoculars, sweeping the sky in all directions. As far as he could see – to all points of the compass – the whole Universe was one enormous but entirely motionless candelabra, except for the barely discernible lights of a strato-cruising jet or two. Traffic lights glow-wormed past on the distant Mumbles Road and below him TVs flickered in a myriad front rooms. He panned away. The only other moving lights were also low down: the two lighthouses – one near, one far – a middle-distance lightship and faintly intermittent shafts of headlamps upward-stabbing from the Devon coast.

The TV was still on when he eventually went back in but all three of them had gone to bed. He sat down on the settee and switched it off. A section of sea and sky was still visible beyond the living room window but with the room and him submersed in the goldfish bowl of it. After a bit, he pulled the poem out of his back pocket, intending to work on it some more but he couldn't bring himself to look at it again. The half-emptied bowl of eggs was still lying there where his wife had left it. It was almost exactly 152 years since the birth of Samuel L. Clemens and 76 years since the death of Mark Twain. He picked an egg out of the bowl, at random, and turned it over in his hand, searching for a sign.

Rhyme, Wine and Worse

The woman rang him mid-evening. Her name was Doris Vane and she was organizing a Poetry and Folk evening in the Grand Lodge, Pontyfelin. She'd heard Perkins wrote poems about workmen and what she had in mind was an evening of poetry and song with the emphasis on the humour of the working man. Pontyfelin, as he probably knew, was a mining area and that sort of evening ought to go down well. She was going to pair him with an ex-Chief Librarian and Local Historian-cum-folk-singer by the name of Handel Rees Hughes. She had it all worked out: Perkins would read for about ten minutes, then Handel would sing for ten minutes, then a couple of miners she knew would read some humorous poems about mining and then, if Perkins didn't mind, she'd like to read one or two of her own poems. Then there'd be a break for food and then Perkins would read for another ten minutes and Handel sing for a further ten, and then there'd be a short open-mike session. It ought to be a really good night – what did Perkins think?

'Sounds good,' he said.

There was a room in the Grand Lodge that could hold up to eighty people and that was the one she was booking. There were lots of people who were interested and she was going to sell tickets at one pound 75 and have a buffet laid on. There were several *'real characters'* she knew of who'd do a spot but the stars of the evening would be Perkins and Handel. The Lounge had a smaller room partitioned off, which had a nice intimate atmosphere and the landlord was a personal friend of hers. She'd already asked Handel and was sure she could get close on eighty people to come. It ought to be a nice evening: Perkins reading a few, then Handel singing, then the miners and then her reading one or two of her own.

'Sounds good!' Perkins said again. He'd been working on a story when she rang and badly wanted to get back to it before he lost the thread.

'Oh I'm so glad you've agreed,' she said. The Regional Arts Association would pay the fees and expenses for the readers and the entry fee would cover the cost of the food. So, it was all settled, then. Did he know how to get to Pontyfelin?

He had to admit he didn't and she spent another half hour giving him directions, which he hastily scribbled down on the inside covers of an old paperback he had handy.

'Well, that's fine,' he said. 'Should be a good night.'

'Should be,' she echoed.

'Thank you for asking me – '

'And thank you for accepting – '

'See you on the 25th, then – '

'Yes – and I look forward to meeting you – '

'Well, goodbye now – '

'Goodbye – and thank you.'

That was the last he heard from her for two months, then a week before the 25th, the phone went again. He was still working on the same story.

'Hello this is Doris Vane,' she said. 'I'm ringing about Friday night – ' Then she went through it all again. There'd been a hitch: Handel had thought it was the 5th October, according to someone she knew who knew him and she'd had an awful job contacting him to tell him the 25th. September. How he'd got the 5th. October she couldn't imagine. There'd been a mix up somewhere but, not to worry, he'd definitely be there. He was getting on a bit and had to travel all the way from up the Valleys, so he'd be staying the night in Pontyfelin and travelling back by bus next morning. Everything else was going according to plan: the room booked, a buffet for eighty arranged, tickets printed, posters posted and fees and expenses forms forwarded by the Arts Association. The miners would read some humorous ones and she'd also read a few of her own.

'I'm glad you rung,' Perkins said. 'Those directions you gave me: I wrote them down on the inside cover of a book and I've forgotten which book it was – '

Friday, he delayed sorting through his poems till the last minute. He half sorted them in the early evening, then rang his father to see if he'd like to go along. His father knew nothing about poetry but enjoyed a pint and a car ride.

They arrived at the Grand Lodge after an erratic hour and a half's drive along tortuous country lanes. They were deliberately early and the place was empty – both Bars – but for the landlord and landlady. Perkins bought two pints and two packets of Solar Crunch and sat down next to his father on a bench. It was a big Lounge – nicely done out – and could easily accommodate eighty people. He started sorting out his poems straightaway and while he was in the middle of it, two big men came in and shouted across to the landlord that they'd got the piano outside.

They went out again and there was the sound of something being bumped and dragged and then the landlord and landlady rushed in and asked if Perkins and his father wouldn't mind moving – they wanted to put the piano where the bench was. The table and bench were hastily moved aside and the two big men struggled in with the piano.

Doris arrived shortly after the piano. She was easily recognizable from her voice and the pile of booklets she was clutching. With her were two men, one of whom Perkins guessed must be Handel. For the sake of the reading, he hoped it was the middle-aged smiling one but, as it turned out, it was the old, hangdog looking one.

He went over and introduced himself to Doris. She was tall and gawky with a long neck, very little chin and pale blue watery eyes – but quite striking, in an odd sort of way. She was glad to see him and hoped it was going to be a good evening and that everyone who'd promised to come *would* come. There was food laid out for eighty people, the piano'd just arrived, there'd been an item on Swansea Sound and everything looked set for eight o' clock.

She laid out the books he'd brought on a table, along with some by Handel and several slim Vanity Press booklets of her own. Handel shook hands limply, looking as though he'd just suffered a bereavement and was shortly expecting to suffer another. The other man was a very important person in those parts, Doris said: the

Personnel Manager of the local colliery. The Personnel Manager's grip was firmer than Handel's and he shrugged off the word 'important' with a careless wave of the hand. Doris ordered a round, which the Personnel Manager insisted on paying for. They all sat round a table, Handel enigmatically silent, upright but slightly bowed at the shoulders, a remote look on his face. Perkins couldn't picture him singing a humorous song but Doris said he knew lots: 'He had a marvellous reception in the Buffalo in Cymer the other night, didn't you, Handel?' she said. Handel nodded slowly.

Everyone felt out of place. The Personnel Manager started asking Perkins questions about inspiration and where it came from and why it was that some people had it and others didn't. Doris seemed to be desperately trying to look intrigued as Perkins found himself talking about Beethoven and his Ode to Joy. His father sat like a stranger listening. Handel hardly moved, but he blinked occasionally and flicked out his tongue chameleon-like to lick his lower lip. The place was suddenly beginning to fill up: two more people had come in, making seven in all.

Doris looked at her watch. 'I do hope people are going to come,' she said. It was ten to eight. Perkins told her not to worry adding, by way of a joke, that he didn't care whether he read to eight or eighty as long as he got his £30 fee.

Handel started to speak after a bit. Everyone looked at him. His mouth had definitely opened and Perkins' father, mis-hearing him, asked how much was his latest book. He had picked up a soft-backed copy of it from the table and, as he asked, was reaching into his pocket. 'Four pounds seventy five,' came the reply, too late for him to withdraw his hand. He handed over a fiver and Handel gave him 25p in return without blinking an eye.

Every time the door opened they all looked round. Doris was looking jittery now. She recited a complete mental list of who she'd asked, which seemed like half the work force of the Pontyfelin colliery. 'Is Winston coming?' the Personnel Manager asked. Doris's eyes lit up: 'Yes, Winston's coming,' she said, 'and he's promised to read some of his grandfather's poems. They're really funny – real, earthy, miners' humour.'

Two people came in and, perhaps catching something of their drift, went straight out again and a man who'd been sitting by the bar, downed his pint and also left. It was ten past eight.

'Doris has put a lot of time and effort into organizing this,' the Personnel Manager said. 'It would be a pity if more didn't turn up. I think we should wait a bit. Give them another quarter of an hour.' They gave them another quarter of an hour and then another ten minutes for luck. Doris got up and drew back some curtains at the far end of the room, revealing a small inner room. At the back of this, running the length of one whole wall, like a Harvest Festival altar in church, was a long table laid out as though for a banquet. She let them feast their eyes on it a moment, then let the curtain drop back.

A tall man with a shock of blond hair and buckteeth came in. 'Here's Winston!' Doris and the Personnel Manager exclaimed in unison. 'You *are* going to read, aren't you, Winston?' Doris said. Winston grinned bashfully: 'I haven't got the book and anyway, it's all in Welsh.'

'Oh, you *must* read – *please*, Winston. You *promised*.'

'Yes. You've got to read. Go and get the book!'

Winston wavered: 'Well, I don't know – '

'*Please*, Winston!'

'Oh all right – I'll go and get the book.' He went and got the book, which must have been just behind the Lounge door because he was back in no time. 'Here it is,' he said, holding it up and grinning.

'Winston's grandfather worked down the mine,' Doris explained. 'He used to keep this diary with poems in it about his experiences. They're *very* funny.'

'It's an historic document,' the Personnel Manager said. 'He ought to try and get it published.'

Winston flicked open the pages. 'Trouble is, it's all in Welsh, though,' he said.

'It doesn't matter,' Doris said. 'Read us a verse or two just to give us the flavour.'

He read a few verses in Welsh, which only the Personnel Manager and Doris understood. They both laughed and then Winston translated. It was a poem about miners emigrating to New Zealand at the time of the General Strike and was, apparently, a lot funnier in the original.

'You ought to get that published,' the Personnel Manager said. 'That's of historical interest.'

'Yes,' everyone echoed. 'That ought to be published.'

It was twenty to nine. Two women came in: one young with big brown eyes and quite pretty and one very young and blond and very pretty. From the way the first one poked her head around the door, Perkins had the impression that she was hoping to find the room empty. Doris greeted them like long lost friends and announced to the gathering that they'd better make a start. The little annexe, she now thought, would be cosier and more than big enough to hold the nine of them. They went in and drew the curtains behind them. The two women sat directly opposite Perkins, the Personnel Manager on his immediate left, his father to his right. Doris said a few words first, then the Personnel Manager got up and spoke for a solid ten minutes before anyone realized that Handel was missing. He was still sitting in the other room, presumably waiting for them all to return. Doris fetched him and parked him next to the two women, where he sat looking small and diminutive.

'What about the piano?' somebody said.

'He sings without it,' Doris said, an unmistakable note of regret in her voice. It was time to start. Everyone coughed and fidgeted and became solemn, as before a sermon. Doris looked to Perkins to begin; Perkins looked at Winston: 'What about Winston?' he said. 'I thought *he* was going to read first.'

'Yes – c'mon, Winston,' said the Personnel Manager, 'You *did* promise.'

'Yes. Fair's fair!'

Winston did his bashful act again, even blushing a bit this time. 'Oh all right then,' he said, at last, 'just one verse then – '

He read and translated two or three pages about miners emigrating to New Zealand during the Depression and once again only

Doris and the Personnel Manager laughed.

Then it was Perkins' turn to read. He'd hoped Winston might have broken the ice but he hadn't even chipped the surface. Perkins read a sequence of what he considered to be some of his most amusing poems but they might as well have been in Urdu for all the response they elicited. The two girls looked slightly wistful, as though they should have been home washing their hair. By the time he was halfway through, the Lounge had started to re-populate behind the curtains and there was a disconcerting buzz of people beginning to enjoy themselves. The landlord could be heard calling for quiet but nobody seemed to be taking much notice. Perkins carried on reading against the growing hubbub and then Doris stopped him abruptly and called on Handel to sing. By now, there was a full-scale party going on in the Lounge.

Handel got up and slowly placed a chair in the middle of the room, which he stood behind, holding on to its back for support. The two girls looked at him with renewed interest imagining, perhaps, that he was about to do a handstand on it. As he opened his mouth to speak, there was a clatter of glasses and a drunken cry from behind the curtains: *'Will Ellis, cut that out –* **now!'** the landlord's voice boomed. *'There's a* **poetry reading** *going on in there!'* A muffled voice slurred something back at him and the noise temporarily abated.

'I'm going to sing a well-known ballad about a man from Pontyfelin who loses his wife in the Lounge Bar of the Colliers Arms, Pontyfelin and sets off to look for her, thinking she has run off with another man. It is intriguing to note how many towns and villages have been successfully interwoven into the story,' Handel announced. He took a deep breath and began singing. His voice, a cracked and quavering baritone, could hardly be heard above the noise from the Lounge. He rocked the chair as he sang:

'"...I searched everywhere in the Rhondda, I declare:
Treherbert, Ystrad, Tonypandy, Porth,
Dinas, Hafod, Llwynpia, Ferndale, Maerdy, Ynyshir.."'

The song was tuneless and went on for ages – an amazing tour-de-force of memory stringing together long lists of place names:

'"...Dowlais, Merthyr, Aberdare,
Pontlottyn, Rhymney, Tredegar, Old and New,
Brynmawr and Ebbw Vale..."'

When he reached Nantyglo, he paused and everyone looked up, hoping he'd found her at last but it was only to get his breath back and off he went again:

'"...all the Western Valleys down, Abercarn and Risca,
Blackwood, Newbridge, Crumlin..."'

Perkins looked across at the girls and could see them exchanging glances:

'"...Pontypool ...Cwmbran...Newport...Cardiff..."'

He couldn't look up now in case he caught the eye of one of them. He was suddenly desperate to laugh, but looked down at his feet and tried hard to think of something else. The Personnel Manager looked discreetly at his watch:

'"...Barry...Cowbridge...Aberavon...Neath..."'

Perkins' whole body was starting to shake, his eyes well with tears. On and on Handel went: Cymmer, Maesteg, Garw, Gilfach, Ogmore Vale, Tondu, Bridgend and eventually, and at long last, back to Pontyfelin, where he found his wife drunk in the Miners Arms. Everyone laughed with relief, Perkins louder and far longer than anyone else – until Handel said he would sing another one. 'This next one's about a pit disaster,' he said. 'It's so pathetic I think I'll sing it all – '

Perkins looked down at his feet. Three youths, with huge tattooed arms, trooped in and trooped back out again. Someone started playing the piano. By the time Handel had finished, half a mining village had been wiped out and it was getting late.

Doris announced that it was time to start on the buffet. She hoped everyone would eat as much as they liked because there was plenty there. Suddenly their number swelled to double figures, everyone jostling and elbowing for position. Halfway through filling his plate, the Personnel Manager turned to Perkins and said: 'I hope you don't mind. My mother in law is very ill. Last week it was my sister in law's turn to look after her, this week it's mine. You know how it is. I'm afraid I'll have to leave at ten fifteen.'

'Of course,' Perkins said, glancing at the time, which was now ten past ten.

Doris came over. 'D'you think you could read something *happy* now?' she said. Perkins was taken aback: he'd already used every funny poem in his repertoire and had only the serious stuff left. He went to the Bar and drank three double rum and blacks in a row, washed down with a pint of lager. When he returned, Doris was just finishing reading from one of her booklets, the small group gathered defensively in a semicircle around her. The noise from the Lounge was now quite deafening and there had been more infiltrators: two miners sat grinning, pints in hand, on the periphery and an enormous woman had wedged herself behind the buffet table and was stuffing sausage rolls into her mouth while simultaneously taking big spoonfuls of everything within reach.

Perkins read one of his most serious poems, glancing up in mid-verse to catch the two girls choking with suppressed laughter. He carried on his reading in an extra loud and monotonous voice, at the end of each poem throwing the typescript up in the air and letting it flutter to the carpet.

'Oh don't do that!' Doris said. 'Please don't throw them away!' She got down on her hands and knees and started picking them up for him.

'Crap!' Perkins said, throwing away the next poem and the next, 'All **crap!**'

'No, they're not.'

'Yes they **are!**'

'Oh please go on. They're good poems, aren't they?' she said, turning to the others. No one said anything, except his father, who muttered something into his pint. 'Yes they are – they're *good* poems,' Doris insisted. 'Please read some more!'

Perkins started another one and threw that up in the air, too: '*You* read one, Doris!' he said.

'No, I'd rather *you* read,' she said. 'After all, it is *your* night…but' – she wavered – 'oh, all right then – ' And completely oblivious to the chaos unleashing itself around her, she picked up a booklet and began reading – trippingly and with perfect enunciation – as though to a Sunday school gathering. Perkins collected up his books and papers, shuffling them together as noisily as he could and stuffing them into his carrier bag. Doris finished reciting, then it was Handel's turn again: *Handel's Last Stand*. Someone gave him a nudge and he rose to his feet hesitantly and stood behind the chair. He needed the words for this next one he said and produced a small diary from which he proceeded to sing in his now familiar monotone. It was another disaster ballad. This time he got halfway through and dried up, his lips working but no sound coming from them. Everyone, except for the fat woman behind the buffet table, poised on his next note but, either because he was suffering a mild catatonic fit or there was a page missing, that note just wouldn't come. One of the two girls was now almost in paroxysms. The landlord's bell clanged, sounding the retreat with Handel still standing there open-mouthed like a ventriloquist's dummy.

'Just time for one more poem,' Doris said to Perkins. Perkins refused point-blank. '*Please*, Alvin,' she begged, 'Just *one* to close. He should read just one more, shouldn't he – ?' she appealed to the others. No one said anything, not even his father. Doris reluctantly conceded defeat and gave a hasty speech of thanks, apologizing for the lack of numbers and the noise. The miners clapped.

The two girls and Winston thanked Doris for a wonderful evening and went out, followed by Doris herself, who said she was just going to settle up with the landlord for the food.

Perkins surveyed the battlefield. His father downed his pint and made his way to the buffet table – where the fat woman was still furiously gorging herself – and slipped a pasty and a Scotch egg into his pocket.

Handel came over, shaking his head as though at news of some further catastrophe at the pit. 'I feel sorry for Doris,' he said. 'She's tried so hard. All that food gone to waste. And the piano. The noise was bad: they couldn't hear – '

Doris returned looking slightly shell shocked. 'I've paid £45 for the food,' she said, 'and made nearly £13 in ticket money. He let me off for the Lounge so I suppose it could have been worse – ' Perkins and Handel commiserated: Perkins, suddenly sober again, offering her his expenses to help out. 'If only the Association had laid on a bus,' Handel said, 'they could probably have filled this place – '

They all gathered up their books and booklets and as they came away, a man strode in from the Lounge and dragged the fat woman away from the food.

It was a bright, moonlit Autumn evening outside. They walked to the car park, Handel still shaking his head: 'I feel bad about this, Doris,' he kept saying. 'The Association should have laid on a bus. If they'd laid on a bus they'd have filled the place. It was full up for me in Cymer last week.'

Doris concurred: 'That's right,' she said. 'He almost brought the house down in Cymer – '

Handel racked his brain for a reason: 'Was there anything else on in Pontyfelin tonight?' he asked. Not that Doris knew of. She'd advertised well in advance in the Pontyfelin Star, there'd been an item on Swansea Sound and posters up all over Town. At least eighty people had promised to come. She just couldn't understand it.

'There's been a lot of flu going about, mind – ' Perkins' father suggested.

'No, that wasn't it,' Perkins said. 'It was just one of those things.'

'Well, *I* enjoyed it,' his father lied.

'So did *I*!' said Perkins, Handel and Doris, almost simultaneously.

They shook hands, everyone apologizing to, or commiserating with, everyone else. They'd all have to get together again before too long, Doris said, and give it another try. But next time would be different. Next time they'd lay on a bus.

Personal Best

He got out of the shower and stood towelling himself in front of her. She looked up from the Cosmopolitan she'd been reading and reached for the toilet roll: 'It's getting smaller,' she said, matter-of-factly. He looked down. She was right: it was definitely getting smaller – two inches, he estimated with the testicles nowhere in sight. He towelled it harder, trying to work back some life.

'It's all that jogging you've been doing,' she said. 'It's wasting away.'

He tried to look unconcerned: 'It's a well known scientific fact,' he said, 'when you run, your testicles retract. Nature's got it all worked out. It's for their own protection. If they didn't they'd get crushed. Did you know that these Sumo wrestlers can retract their testicles at will – push them right up inside themselves? You look carefully next time they're on TV. They've been doing it for thousands of years.'

She wasn't convinced. She kept looking at it as though it was about to drop off. 'The boys'll put you to shame: Mathews' is about that long,' she said, showing him with her fingers, 'and you should see Owain's – it's huge. Longer than this toilet roll.'

'Mine is,' he said. 'When roused. It must be from lack of use.'

The sarcasm hit home: 'Don't blame me,' she snapped. 'I asked you to come to bed yesterday but you wanted to go out jogging. Look at it – it's shrivelling away!'

He stood there trying to think of something sexy but it didn't grow any bigger. You could hardly tattoo *Love* on it any more, let alone *Love is a Many Splendoured Thing*.

She got up and flushed the toilet. 'Come in the shower with me,' he said.

'No thanks,' she said, patting her stomach in front of the mirror, 'You've just had one – and, anyway, I think there's something wrong with me: I shouldn't be this big.'

He put his arms around her and she pushed him away, cursing

loudly. 'Shhh!' he said. 'They can hear everything next door. These walls are paper thin.'

'I don't care,' she said.

'Nor me,' he said, hopelessly. 'They've heard it all by now, anyway.'

After she'd gone, he stood on the scales in front of the mirror and was pleased to find that he'd lost three and a half pounds on the run he'd just made. He went in the bedroom and lay on the bed trying to work his testicles back into position but lying down only made them retract even further. He got up and tried to coax them back in the standing position but to no avail. Downstairs, he filled in his Runner's Log:

7.30p.m. 11 miles. Cenotaph to Lighthouse and back: 1hr.15.20. P.B. Pushed all the way. Wind westerly. Wt. 11.3. Pulse 48. Balls disappeared.

Snow

For a moment Perkins didn't know where he was or what time it was. The dream he'd had seemed to have gone on for ever but he couldn't remember a single word or image of it. He was sure there must have been snow in it, though, because there was snow in the late night film that was still showing on TV. He had no idea when it had fallen – certainly not before he'd fallen asleep – but there were two men in the middle of nowhere, silently digging away at a snowdrift. He didn't know where they'd come from or where they were trying to get to. Their breath curled about the screen as they worked and the sound of their shovels scraping on tarmac echoed round the room. He watched for a moment, wondering who they could be but they didn't speak, they just kept on shovelling in total silence. After a bit, he got tired of waiting, switched them off and went upstairs to bed.

Snow was forecast in actuality. According to the Weatherman, it was moving in, at that very moment, from the Steppes. And he was desperately hoping it would because that coming evening he had to give a poetry reading in a remote little valley town, way out in the wilds.

He'd already undressed, got into bed and switched off the light, before he heard the distant murmur of voices. It was from his wife's portable TV in the other bedroom. He wondered if it could be the two men still digging, but if it was them they must have dug a way through by then because there was no scraping of shovels to be heard, just a low, muffled conversation.

He was in two minds whether to go in or not. They weren't talking very loudly but loud enough to keep him awake. He turned over and pulled the sheet up over his head but it was no good and in the end he got up and went into her room. The voices had stopped by the time he got there – replaced by a high-pitched bleep – and the small screen, two feet from her pillow, was snowing.

He tiptoed across to turn down the sound but stumbled on a shoe and her eyes immediately opened. She saw snow first and then him.

'What d'you want?' she said.

'I was just going to switch the TV off, love,' he said. 'You're not watching it, are you?'

'No, I was sleeping.'

'Shall I switch it off?'

'No, leave it.'

'There's nothing on. I'll switch it off and come in with you, if you like.'

She looked confused – still feverish from the flu she'd been suffering from for the last four or five days – unable to think straight. 'What's the matter?' she said. 'Why are you here?'

He sat down on the bed, leaned forward and was about to embrace her. 'You fell asleep on me again tonight,' she said. 'That's every night this week. I think you need to see a doctor. You've got tired blood or something. And why have you come in now? Have you had a bad dream? Did you dream I died or something?'

He straightened up. 'No – but I did have a dream,' he said. 'Downstairs on the settee. A helluva long one – full of images but I can't remember a single one. It was one of those dreams that just goes on and on. I think there may have been snow in it – '

She looked at him, trying to read something into his expression: 'Why are you coming in to me now? Why are you bothering me like this?' He didn't know what to say. It was really only to switch off the TV – nothing more, nothing less – but, in her confused state, she seemed determined to read more into it. 'I know why,' she said, 'It's the reading, isn't it? You're shit-scared about the reading tomorrow and now you're coming in to me for reassurance. There's always an ulterior motive. Is that it? Are you shitting yourself about the reading?'

'Shitting myself? Of course not,' he laughed. 'Readings never bother me any more. In any case the weather forecast looks bad. There's a front moving in from Russia – from the Steppes, according to the Weatherman. It'll probably be cancelled.'

'Well, you'd better go back in there,' she said, 'I'm too hot and my breathing's still not right. Stay in there tonight.'

He got up to go. It was just as well. She'd put all the pillows under her head anyway and he was feeling pretty restless himself. As he got up, he reached for a knob on the TV: 'D'you mind if I turn the sound down a bit then?' he said.

'Just leave it,' she said.

He left it, not for one moment questioning why she would want to watch – or listen to – a screen-full of static. But as he opened the door to go she said, 'What date is it?'

'The sixth,' he said. 'Why?'

She thought for a moment. 'When did my father die?'

He had to think: 'The sixth,' he said. '– eighteen years ago.'

'Eighteen years to the day,' she said, still staring at the screen. 'Almost to the hour. It doesn't seem possible, does it? It's like only yesterday.'

Eighteen years. Yes, she was right: it really didn't seem possible. He wanted to say something consolatory but it came out as an all-too-crass: 'Christ – time flies, doesn't it!'

Then he went back into the other room, got into bed and put out the light. But he could still hear the high-pitched bleep of the portable. He tossed and turned for a while, then got up and tiptoed back into her room. She was already asleep, blind to the glare of the cathode rays, her pale face lit by a terrible blizzard of snow...

Night on a Bare Mountain

Perkins woke abruptly with his wife digging him in the ribs. There was some sort of anthropological documentary on BBC2 but, much to her annoyance, he'd kept dozing off. 'That's a coincidence,' she was saying, 'this programme's all about the Incas and that little ocarina I bought in the Charity Shop this morning is from Peru – !'

Perkins didn't know what she was on about at first and then he remembered the little artefact he'd picked up off the kitchen table earlier in the day. It was made of brightly painted terra cotta, like half a castanet, and had six holes in it. He'd put it to his lips and puffed and blown into each hole in turn until he was red in the face but couldn't get a sound out of it. He'd had to sit down in the end because the strain had made him dizzy. His wife was going to give it as a Christmas present to her friend Geena.

She cracked him a nut from the bowl of nuts she'd been saving for Christmas and they sat for a while eating and watching the rest of the programme. But then, half-way through the fall of the Inca Empire, Perkins switched channels: 'Only for a minute,' he assured her. 'There's something I want to see – ' It was a documentary about a Mountain Rescue team, a reconstruction of a real-life rescue of a man who'd gone hiking alone on a remote Scottish mountain and got lost in a blizzard. It had got dark and he'd had to dig himself a hole in the snow to survive.

She cracked two more nuts and handed him one. 'Geena's up on the mountain tonight,' she said, matter-of-factly.

'What's she doing up there?' he said.

'Don't you remember me telling you? She's got to go up the mountain and spend the night on her own. It's the Celtic New Year tonight. She's got to perform various ceremonies up there. It's part of the process of Healing the Land – and herself.'

Perkins ate the nut and held out his hand for another. The Reconstruction search party were out with flares and torches in the driving snow. It looked like an impossible task. 'Has she got a portable TV?' he said.

'Don't be daft,' she said. 'The whole point is that she goes up there alone, with nothing but a torch and a sleeping bag. She's going to ring me between nine and ten tomorrow morning to let me know she's alright. If she doesn't, I've got to alert her son...What are you smiling at?'

Perkins hadn't realized he was. 'It's just the thought of Geena lying up there alone on a night like this,' he said. 'The weather forecast's terrible. Where is she exactly?'

'Somewhere on top of the Brecon Beacons,' she said, handing him a nut, 'but only I know exactly where. It's a beautiful spot right out in the wilds. It took her a long time to find it. She's very brave. I don't think I could do it. And it's not the first mountain she's been up, either – she's been up lots.'

'What happens if she's ill and you die in the night,' he said. 'No one will know she's there.'

'If I die in the night, you ring her son. Let him know what's happened. He'll know what to do.'

Perkins still couldn't help smiling and thinking how lucky he was. It was cold outside and heavy snow was forecast but inside it was warm and snug on the settee in front of the telly, with the fire blazing, the faery lights glowing, a fridgeful of Old Speckled Hen and the Late Film due on at any minute. He was glad to be where he was and yet part of him envied Geena, wanted to be out there among the elements on top of some remote mountain, far from the trappings of civilization, feeling the grass grow under him, looking up at the blackness, healing the land – and, who knows, maybe his soul as well. He popped another nut.

They forgot all about Geena then. The rescuers were within reach. The hiker was just about to give up all hope of ever being dug out, when Perkins' wife said: 'Put it back on the Incas, now.'

'Just let me see the actual rescue first – ' he said, but she was already clicking away at the remote. He grabbed the other remote and started clicking, too: *the Incas versus the Conquistadores and Mountain Rescue:* and before either of them knew it, one thing led to another and there were nuts and crackers and remotes flying everywhere and he was storming out of the house in a rage.

He was halfway down the steps before she realized he'd gone and then he heard her voice sailing out after him, loud and clear on the frosty air: 'That's it, go on: **run away!** You've been **running away** all your life – but don't expect me to be here when you get back...'

Her voice trailed off as he hurried on down the street, avoiding the glance of a startled neighbour, pretending the voice had nothing at all to do with him, or the loud report as the front door, with its wreath of mistletoe, slammed shut with a shuddering finality.

When he reached the corner lamp, he felt in his pockets and cursed. No money. No Visa card. And no key to his studio. He was always doing that: storming out of the house without first checking if he had about him the basic means for survival. Now he couldn't even drown his sorrows over a Festive pint. It was the bleak midwinter and he'd been in such a hurry he hadn't even grabbed his coat on the way out.

It had been a totally unnecessary argument, as most of their arguments were, but once it had started there'd been no turning back. And if he'd stayed a second longer he knew, from bitter experience, things would probably have gone from bad to worse.

Two or three streets later, he'd started to cool down a bit but was already beginning to feel the first pangs of loneliness and remorse. He tried to see into lighted windows as he passed: a Christmas tree or two, artificial snow, tinsel, flickering blue blurs behind net curtains…

He buttoned his shirt right up to the collar and dug his hands deep in his pockets. He couldn't go far dressed as he was. There were blizzards on the way and he was freezing already. He needed shelter and sustenance, somewhere to sit down and collect his thoughts, give his wife time to collect hers.

There were picnic benches on the grass of a recreation area at the end of a nearby lane. He sat down on one of them but there was a cold wind blowing directly from the sea and he soon moved on.

The adjoining quarry was more sheltered, lit only faintly by the amber glow of the estate which was set back on top of it. He nearly always ended up here after an argument. It was where they walked sometimes: a lightly wooded area, with a single, circular path, designed and built as a BMX racing track for the local kids.

It was a pleasant walk for a Sunday afternoon but the place was desolate now: a dark, unfathomable hole at the heart of the Town. He stood in the centre of it. Water cascaded down through a crack in the quarry walls, splashing into bottomless pools.

Several weeks before, in daylight, he and his wife had come this way and she'd spotted a fallen tree – little more than a sapling – lying flat out at the side of a pool. The roots were still in the ground but, over a period, the pounding from the water must have loosened the tree and eventually toppled it. She'd wanted him to rescue it: to prop it upright so that it would have a chance to grow back again. She hated to see anything that could be saved, just left to die – and *everyone* had a duty towards the environment. He'd tried to reach the tree there and then but had expensive shoes on and there were brambles and mud to be negotiated. His wife had been upset and disappointed to have to leave it lying there like that. 'Don't worry,' he'd assured her, 'I'll come back in old clothes and do it tomorrow…'

But he hadn't. And he probably never would have, if he hadn't come upon it again now in the darkness – still there beneath the falling water, held by the same few umbilical cords of stringy sap, somehow, after all that time, still clinging on.

When he left the path to take a closer look, it felt like he was stepping into a Neanderthal diorama. The tree was half in half out of an alcove – a shallow cave set in the quarry wall. Sabre-tooth icicles hung overhead. He stamped down some hoary undergrowth and put one foot gingerly on the bank. He thought he could see a way of reaching it – if he held on to another smaller tree and then another…He took his time, gauging every step, feeling in the blackness for firm ground. When he was close enough, he bent down and tried to lift the tree but it was glued down by a thin layer of ice. He tugged it free but it was heavier than he'd thought and the branches were lopsided and slippery. Water splashed at his feet. It would be impossible to re-bury the roots in the dark without some sort of implement so, instead, he searched around for some stones and found several big ones lying in the water. He rested the tree carefully against the quarry wall and bent to pick one up. His hands were numb by now and as he turned with it and stepped back up the bank, his feet slid from under him and down he went. Water flooded his shoes and showered down on his head and shoulders. He slipped and slithered several more times in trying to right himself but, eventually, managed to prop the stone against the foot of the tree. He fetched four or five other stones and propped them against it, too, and by the time he'd finished, the tree was free-standing again.

He hurried back, soaked through and covered in mud, intent on patching things up with his wife, eager to tell her how he'd bought himself some unexpected redemption by helping to heal the land…

It had started to snow by the time he got there but he didn't go in straight away. He stood on the steps in the back yard looking in. She was sitting down by the kitchen table and, although he couldn't see her face properly, he could tell straightaway that she'd been crying. She was hunched in an attitude of total dejection, leaning forward with her head between her hands. He couldn't understand it: the argument had been a fairly run-of-the-mill, storm-in-a-teacup sort of thing and he hadn't expected her to be *that* upset for *that* long. It was cold and miserable out there in the snow and he felt like an escaped convict but it was too soon to go in just yet. He had to get his timing right, otherwise the whole thing could erupt again in recriminations.

The flakes got thicker and thicker, sticking to his eyelashes, carpeting the yard. After a while, their cat came padding out of nowhere, jumping up on the window sill to join him, silently staring in. As they watched, his wife sat up suddenly and wiped her eyes. Then she picked up the little Peruvian ocarina, which was still lying on the table where he'd left it that morning, and put it to her lips. When she blew, miraculously, a long, lone, high-pitched note came out of it, full of a primitive sadness…

Upside Down Roses

He woke from a terrible dream to an ancient situation comedy on the portable TV. It was mid-morning Thursday, the day outside grey and dull through the gap in the curtains. He slotted into her warm back – 66 position – and adjusted the pillow. The film was lousy: a Cro Magnon comedian he'd never heard of before. He didn't know whether she was watching or not. He tried to coax her around with his free hand but she groaned and shrugged him off.

The dream started to come back to him: he was sitting in the car in a car park with his wife and son, when a fighter plane zoomed low overhead. It was heading for the Town but, all of a sudden, looped the loop and came back on itself, bee lining straight for them: *'Duck!'* he just had time to yell as the plane screamed down and dipped from sight behind a nearby bank. There was a split second's pause then an explosion followed by an enormous fireball. Debris flew high in the air: huge chunks of engine and fuselage sailing down in slow motion...When the danger had passed, he went to have a look. The wreckage was well ablaze but, miraculously, there were three survivors coming towards him up the bank: a woman, a little girl and one other person he couldn't quite make out. *'How many still in there!'* he shouted to the woman as he raced to the rescue. 'Two,' she said. 'but they're both dead!' He stopped in his tracks and walked back to the car where his wife and son were anxiously waiting. Next minute, the rescue services arrived. They put the fire out and extricated the bodies. As they dumped them into a big box, the surviving girl became hysterical. Then he'd woken up. It was a ghastly dream. He began to trace back the elements of it to his conscious state, going over it slowly, bit by bit, rationalizing. He wouldn't have got the bodies out in time anyway, he concluded – the plane would have gone up. But he'd have had a go. The two bodies had fallen like rag dolls into the big box. They shouldn't have let the girl stay. Someone should have led her off. It was she who had woken him up. She wouldn't stop screaming...

His wife stirred, rolled over to face him, eyes still shut.

'Give us a kiss,' he whispered.

She puckered her lips mechanically, like a dehydrated jelly fish. 'A romantic one,' he said.

'I can't breathe this morning,' she groaned and rolled back over again.

He smoothed her arm, running his fingers over it, imagining the hairs as trees on a hill, gently mowing them down. A lorry rattled by outside. He lay studying the wallpaper. It was a rose pattern but all the roses were upside down. He hadn't noticed when putting it up. He'd brought his mother up to look two weeks before she died. 'I think I've put it up upside down,' he'd said. 'Yes, you have,' she'd replied, with what he'd thought later was a note of foreboding in her voice. Perhaps it was unlucky? Like broken mirrors or pictures falling off walls. Perhaps it was unlucky for the first visitor to notice upside down wallpaper.

He got up first, made himself breakfast, listened to the radio. There was a *Down Your Way* programme on. A Souvenir Shopkeeper from Tenby wanted Marlene Dietrich singing 'Lili Marlene' as his record request, in memory of all the pals he'd made during his army days. She sang it in German and, as he washed the dishes, Perkins felt a sudden lump form in his throat. Augustus John was born in Tenby, a Town Councillor informed the presenter and a very famous mathematician: the man who invented the 'equals' sign. 'The *equals* sign?' repeated the presenter, *'really?'* A local fisherman came on and explained that although tope were frequently eaten on the Continent, fishermen in those parts wouldn't touch anything that hadn't got scales. He was followed by a monk from Caldey who explained in a tired, unworldly voice, how monks made a living.

Perkins didn't know what to do with himself. He went upstairs, washed, shaved off two days' growth of whiskers, cleaned his teeth and combed his hair. The wasp he'd killed the day before still lay on the window sill next to a pile of old razor blades. He nudged it with a broken piece of bathroom tile but it didn't budge. It was a quarter to twelve. The dog jumped up, sniffing the front door when he put on his jacket but Perkins went out alone.

He strolled indecisively through the back streets. The beach was deserted, the tide halfway in or halfway out. He paused to look in an Estate Agents window and then at the prices in the window of a new Steak House. The menu was accompanied by colour snapshots of the inside tastefully done out with, in the corner of one, a sloe, doe-eyed waitress backed anxiously against a table.

There was cricket on in the Trafalgar. He hadn't been in there for years. What had once been three or four separate bars had been knocked into one split-level one and there were now false timbers all around the place in half-hearted imitation of the Flagship Victory. There were only two or three regulars spectating at the counter and a middle-aged couple sitting in the only two seats that looked out to sea. Perkins bought a half and went and sat on the lower deck next to the jukebox. He selected a couple of records, including an old Beatles' one, then took out his notebook and began writing in it. After a while, he became aware of a woman sitting on her own on the other side of the room. She seemed quite pretty from where he was sitting but, without his glasses on, fuzzy. As he wrote, he glanced over at her occasionally.

The poem he was trying to write didn't want to be written. He was about to give up when, out of the blue, she came over to him, smiling. 'Excuse me,' she said. 'I saw you sitting there all on your own and I wondered whether you'd like to come over and join us – I'm on my own, too, for the moment. My friend's gone somewhere and I'm not sure when she's coming back. She just seems to have disappeared.'

Perkins half rose, hesitated. Close-up she looked completely different. 'Come on over,' she coaxed. 'You don't want to sit there on your own.'

It was too late to do anything else: 'Okay,' he said and followed her across the room with his glass and notebook. They sat down, both smiling uneasily. 'D'you want a drink?' he said, pointing to an empty glass in front of them. 'My friend's,' she said, picking up her half full glass from the adjacent table. 'She's supposed to be coming back in a minute but she seems to have disappeared. D'you come here often?'

'Occasionally,' he said, suddenly remembering whom she reminded him of: Ruth Ellis, the last woman to be hung. Same sort of hairstyle and colouring – only older.

'Married?'

'Yes,'

'Living with your wife?'

'Yes. And you?'

Divorced. I hope you don't think I was brazen asking you across like that.'

'No, not at all.'

'D'you live around here?'

'On the hill. And you?'

'Brynmill – but I'm from Liverpool originally.'

'*Liverpool!*' Perkins said. 'I just put a Beatles' number on the jukebox but it hasn't come on yet.'

'I like the Beatles,' she sighed. 'I was sad when John Lennon was shot.'

'So was I. I couldn't believe it. Did you ever meet them?'

'No. The only one I knew was Cilla Black's husband. I knew him quite well.'

'Did you ever go to the Cavern or was that before your time?'

'Good God, how old d'you think I am?'

'Forty-five?'

'Thank you.'

'Older or younger?'

'I'm fifty-one.'

'So am I. What month were you born?'

'January.'

'You're older than me. I'm March but you don't look fifty-one.'

'Thanks. What d'you do?'

'What d'you think?'

'I don't know.'

'Nothing. I *was* a teacher.'

'A teacher!'

'Don't I look like one?'

'I don't know. I just saw you writing. I didn't know what you did.'

He was about to tell her that he was a writer as well, when a second woman – old enough to be her mother – came in and sat down opposite them. The first woman leant forward to talk to her: 'Where've you *been*?' she said, with barely suppressed anger. The old woman began to explain. Perkins looked the other way, relieved now of an excuse for an exit. 'Oh well,' he said, emptying his glass and getting up as casually as he could, 'got to be going now. I'll be seeing you – '

She seemed to have resigned herself to the move as soon as the old woman had appeared: 'Yes,' she said, lamely. 'Goodbye – '

When he got home, with two Indian takeaways, his wife was watching the afternoon film. He waited until she was halfway through the meal and said matter-of-factly: 'I was nearly picked up in the pub just now – ' She didn't divert her gaze. '– by this bird,' he continued. 'This blond came over and started chatting me up. Cracking piece. From Liverpool. Used to know Cilla Black's husband – '

His wife went on eating and watching the film. He wasn't sure whether she'd heard him or not. He thought she must have, but he didn't repeat himself.

That night *he* didn't feel like it. His back was to her's and he was reading but, out of the blue, she reached across and started fondling his ear. He didn't shrug her off, but he didn't respond either. He let her fingers wander down his spine, across and over his thigh then he clamped her hand down with an elbow and she gave up. He felt sorry, almost immediately, but he just didn't feel like it.

Later, he turned to her in the dark but she was sleeping and beyond revival.

He had a funny dream after. He was in some kind of dormitory complex about to go to bed. There were people all around him changing and his bunk was the top one of three. He was one of the last in and he climbed up to it quietly trying hard not to wake anyone. Suddenly, the whole bunk collapsed, showering debris on the bunk underneath. The matron came in and played hell with him.

He abandoned the ruined bunk and went to look for his wife. He searched all the bunks and eventually found her. She went with him to look for somewhere where they could bed down together but wherever they went there were people around. Once, they lay down on the carpet in front of a blazing open fire and were about to make love when they noticed an old man sitting in an armchair watching them. They got up and went to look for somewhere else but there was nowhere to go – nowhere at all.

In the morning, neither of them felt like it. Before he had a chance to recount his dream she told him hers.

'My father came in here last night,' she said, 'and stood there looking at you. He came in twice. He came in and went out, then he came back in again after and stood there looking at you.'

'Did he say anything?'

'No, he just looked.'

'That's odd. How did he look?'

'Sad.'

'You should have woken me. I'd like to have seen him.'

She turned over, hurt: 'That's not funny,' she said. 'You've got to make a joke out of everything, haven't you? If you'd dreamed it was your mother it would be different.'

He lay there, sorry, wishing he'd shut up, knowing nothing he could say would make amends. If he even touched her now, she'd shrink away like a sea anemone. He stared down at the foot of the bed, trying to imagine her father standing there watching them, infinitely sad against the pink and white upside-down roses of the wallpaper.

Mort Dies

Mort was dead and Wales had lost one of its finest and most outspoken poets, lamented the South Eastern Mail at the bottom of its front page, alongside a rather grainy photo of Mort, looking slightly hung-over and a lot older than his forty-odd years.

Perkins' wife was frying some bacon when he broke the news to her. She didn't look up from the frying pan: 'It says here he died in his sleep sometime yesterday morning, after a poetry reading in West Wales. He'd been a guest reader at the Llandewifanog Soroptomist Society's Annual Christmas Dinner – ' Perkins put the paper down: *'Christ!* I read to *them* once,' he exclaimed. 'No wonder he bloody died.'

His wife flipped the bacon onto a plate and handed it to him. 'Are you surprised he's dead?' she said.

Perkins had to admit he wasn't, although he hadn't spoken to Mort for almost six years. He'd last read with him at a Club in Tylerstown, when he'd had occasion to physically accost Mort after overhearing him disparage his poetry during the interval. He'd almost bumped into him several times since then but, on each occasion, Mort had either been going into or coming out of a pub and he'd managed to avoid him. He'd liked Mort and his work – a lot – but drink and Mort and him didn't mix. It was as simple as that.

Perkins spread the newspaper beside his plate on the kitchen table and sat down to eat. 'What did he die of?' his wife asked.

'It doesn't say – heart by the sound of it.'

'Too much or too little?'

'I knew you'd make a joke,' Perkins said. 'You never liked him much, did you?'

'I never liked him when he was drunk,' she said. 'Sober, you couldn't meet a nicer man.'

The funeral was held a few days later at a crematorium in Mort's home town of Cwmhowell. Perkins took a day off work to go. He'd never been to Cwmhowell before, so allowed himself plenty of time for the combined train and bus journey. In the event, he arrived too early. Cwmhowell turned out to be a depressing ex-coal-mining town tucked away at the Heads of the Valleys. It was a blustery March day and the first thing that struck him when he got off the bus was the unmistakable smell of crematorium smoke. He hurried to the nearest pub – the only pub, as it turned out – that served a bleak council estate, miles from anywhere.

It was quite a smart, refurbished-looking place inside with a thriving clientele. Perkins looked around for any fellow mourners he might know. Two men, standing at the end of the bar, were staring across at him as he called his pint. He thought for a moment they might be Press or even poets but it soon became apparent that they were neither. Their eyes followed him as he took his pint and sat down at a nearby table. The shorter man said something and the taller one laughed out loud: *'Mort!'* he said, above the murmur of the Bar, 'I'll tell you what *Mort* was: e was a bastard. An out-and-out **bastard!**'

Perkins sipped at his pint as though he had other things on his mind but he could tell the two men were watching his every move. He opened his South Eastern Mail and began to read, determined not to take the bait. 'When I saw that in the paper last week,' the taller one said, in a voice a couple of decibels higher: **'ARTHUR MORT IS DEAD,** I thought: *Thank Christ for that!* E was an orrible man. **Orrible!'**

Perkins turned a page and went on reading. 'E came in ere once,' the taller one persisted, 'I'll *never* forget it: an got into an argument with a guy sittin in a wheelchair – a *cripple!* An d'you know what Mort done? E upped with his glass an threw it at this poor bugger. There was pandemonium in ere! I grabbed im and so did a couple of others an we wrestled im out into the car park. E was like a wild animal, shoutin an swearin all the way: "I'm a poet! I'm Arthur Mort, the poet!" e kept shoutin. "I don't care oo the **fuck** you are," I said. "Jus *don't* come back – drunk or sober!" What a despicable man! What an **evil** bastard!'

Perkins took out his pen and started doing the crossword, aware of two pairs of eyes, through the bar room fug, boring into him. The two men were momentarily silent waiting, in vain, for a reaction. Then the second one said, with even greater relish: 'Yes. The *best news* I'd ad in a long time was when I learnt that e was dead. The **best** news in a long time – !'

Perkins had had enough. He downed his pint, rolled up his newspaper and strode over to the bar. The two men froze, pints poised...but he only smiled at them, plonked down his glass on the counter, thanked the barman and left.

It was a short walk from pub to Crematorium. Little groups of Mort's friends and admirers had already gathered but Perkins didn't feel like socializing. He went and had a look at the wreaths spread out on a grassy verge in front of the chapel, checked that his own had arrived and, for the first time, began to question whether his Fitzgerald quote: *'And some we loved the loveliest and best...'* was maybe a shade over the top. A couple of other writers came to look as well and one of them came over and spoke to him. It seemed that Mort had died on someone else's floor, sometime in the early hours of the morning after the reading, a burnt-out cigarette in one hand, a half-empty can of Murphy's in the other. The TV was still on and, some time during the night, he'd graffiti-ed a banner-sized note to his Soroptomist hostess on the wallpaper above his head: **'THANKS FOR A WONDERFUL PARTY!'**

The chapel was cram-packed and some people had to wait outside. Everybody who was anybody on the Welsh Literary scene seemed to be there and many others besides. Orations were given by two distinguished old Gentlemen-of-Letters. They praised Mort's compassion, humanity and wit as well as the enduring quality of his work, a selection of which was read. Several people had tears in their eyes. Wanting to avoid the end-of-service crush, Perkins left discreetly during the last hymn, the singing fading away behind him as he passed through the outer gates.

It was a dismal return journey. The smell of putrefaction followed him all the way.

The house was empty when he got back. His wife had gone for

a Relaxation session and there was a note on the kitchen table asking him to tidy up and have a cup of tea ready for her by the time she got back.

The stench of the Crematorium was still in his nostrils as he lay down on the settee with a can of beer and one of Mort's books, which he'd plucked at random from a shelf. He hadn't bothered making tea or even switching on a light. He read for a bit and then pulled out a notebook and pen and tried to write something of his own – something about the day he'd had – but it got dark before long and he gave up and switched on the TV.

He clicked through the channels until he chanced upon a programme about computers and poetry. An inventor with literary leanings had come up with a programme that could write poetry. All you had to do was press a button and it would start composing. No self-respecting poet, it seemed, could afford to be without one. You fed it the words and in no time at all, sentences and whole stanzas even, emerged from the printer. No more agonizing. No more angst. You could sit back and let the computer do all the work. Perkins sat there, imagining what Mort – who'd written scathingly about consumerism, 'progress' and the death of old communities – would have to say about it all…

Just as he was about to switch channels, a light came on in the kitchen. He called out, thinking it was his wife come home, but nobody answered. He called out again and, when there was still no answer, got up cautiously and went and checked the back door. It was locked. He checked the Lounge, bedrooms and bathroom and then came back downstairs and checked the light switch, flicking it on and off a couple of times to see if it was faulty. Puzzled and a bit unnerved, he went back in the front room, where the inventor was just starting to recite some of the computer-generated poems. They definitely weren't going to win any prizes but in due course, the inventor promised, the programme would become even more sophisticated and the computer would recite its own poems.

Perkins took out his notebook and pen again, switched off the TV and went and lay on the window seat with his beer. The Irish Ferry was just passing the Mumbles Head on its outward journey.

Clouds, with amber underbellies, hung over the Town. Although the room was in total darkness now, he thought he could write something by touch and feel alone. After all, it was all there, waiting to be down-loaded – from brain to hand to paper – at the mere press of Return: the death of a bygone friend, a long train journey, a funeral…After a while, he gave up on the page and began composing sentences in his head – confused and conflicting ones, in no particular sequence: ways of telling his wife about his day: the two men in the pub, the funeral orations, the TV programme, his unshakeable gloom, the light coming on of its own accord…

Dowsers

When he woke he was alone in the room with the TV still on and the cat asleep on his chest like a feline succubus. He flicked off the set with the remote and sat there, listening. There was nothing to hear. The house was dead still. After a bit, he got up, put the cat on the settee, the guard in front of the fire, the lights out and made his way to bed.

At the sound of his feet on the stairs, his wife came out of the front room. She looked sheepish: as though he'd disturbed her at some clandestine activity. 'I thought you'd gone to bed,' he said. 'What've you been doing in there: performing some diabolical, shamanistic rite or other?'

She seemed reluctant to say at first. 'If you really want to know,' she said, 'I've been dowsing again. Come and see.'

It was late and he was tired but he followed her back into the front room anyway. She took the crystal pendant from around her neck and held it up. 'I've been dowsing different things,' she said, 'to see if they should be here or not. If the crystal moves when I hold it over something, it's okay; if it doesn't move, the object's giving out negative energy and I need to get rid of it. I've identified a few negative things already. Mostly Car Boot Sale stuff: this little pot, that wooden candlestick holder, those blue doilies, the fossil.' She'd made a little heap of them on the table.

'What're you going to do with them all?' Perkins said.

'Put them outside for the time being,' she said. 'Then maybe I ought to bury them. What d'you think?'

He sat down in an armchair. Since it was mostly her stuff she'd weeded out, he didn't have very strong views about it one way or the other, but there was one object he particularly wanted to keep. 'It's up to you,' he said. 'But I *would* like to keep that fossil. It's an ammonite. It's not worth much but it's from that little junk shop we went to in Lymme Regis. It's got sentimental value. We spent a nice day there, once. Remember?'

She remembered but she still didn't think they should keep it. 'I don't know what it is about it,' she said, 'but it's giving out bad energy, look – 'She held the crystal over the fossil and, sure enough, the crystal wouldn't react. 'See what I mean?' she said.

Perkins didn't argue the point. The bad energy must have come from its previous owner, though, because he was sure they'd had a good time that day in Lymme Regis.

The cat jumped up on his chest and lay there. They both watched Perkins' wife as she carried on dowsing: vases, plates, bowls, figurines, innumerable years of accumulated knick-knacks. She paid particular attention to the mantelpiece. Stacked on it, in a rocky little outcrop were all her souvenirs and keepsakes and talismans from wherever in the world they happened to have been: New York, Toronto, Cairo, Luxor, Knossos, Masada, Jerusalem…Stones and feathers and shells and fragments of wood and glass, picked up on beaches and mountain-tops, in temples and parks and palaces all over the Western Hemisphere: some immediately identifiable by country and place, others whose origins had become clouded in the mists of time. But all of them come together there on the black, cast-iron mantelpiece, to work their silent alchemy. And in the middle, like the Patron Saint of Bric-a-brac, was a big, beneficent Buddha, bought in a weak moment in a little Craft shop in the Mumbles. 'This is like my own little altar,' she said. 'You ought to have one as well. There's all these stones you brought back from Long Island and Arles and Egypt on the side here. You should put them together in one spot and make a kind of shrine of them, like I've done.'

He closed his eyes for a moment and his mind wandered back, not to America or France or Africa or any of those distant lands but to a sunny Dorset beach where a couple of middle-aged trippers down from Wales, were strolling arm in arm along the promenade… When he opened them again, his wife was sitting at the table, this time dowsing a photograph. He watched her for a while through half-closed lids while, at the same time, smoothing the cat. She seemed to be concentrating very hard. Sometimes the crystal moved and sometimes it didn't. 'This woman's name was Elizabeth

Hannah Johns,' she said at last, holding the photograph up for him to see. He recognized it as an old sepia one that had been in an album for years. It was of a young woman in a White Edwardian dress, standing next to a big vase of roses. The photo had come from her grandmother's house ages before but, until that moment, nobody in her family had been able to identify the mystery woman. 'How d'you know that?' Perkins said.

'I asked her,' she said. 'It's signed E.H. Johns. I asked if the E was for Elizabeth and the H was for Hannah and she said yes. The crystal moved when I asked. I've found out quite a lot about her while you've been sitting there. She wasn't married. She was a singer. And she was English – from Crouch End.'

'That's amazing!' Perkins said. 'What made you ask her if she was from Crouch End?'

'It's got Crouch End printed on the back,' she said. 'That's where the photographic studio was. I put two and two together. She must have known my grandmother through singing in the same choir as her. I'd like to find out more. This really ought to go back to her family but they may not be there any more. What else can I ask her?'

Perkins was too tired to think. 'How about asking if she knows next week's Lottery numbers?' he said. She ignored this and looked around for something else to dowse but seemed, momentarily, to have run out of possibilities. There was only the big stuff left. Undeterred, she began dowsing one of his paintings, which was lying on the settee. Then a vase of bright red tulips. Then the settee itself. The table. An oil lamp. All, to his great relief, were positive. Finally, she sat down on a chair, exhausted.

'Dowse *this* then,' he said, on a whim, holding out his hand.

'What's the point in dowsing that?' she said.

'To reassure me.'

'Of *what?*'

'Of its ability to still write good poems.'

She went over to him and dangled the crystal above his palm for a good half minute, but nothing happened. In desperation, he vibrated his hand – ever so slightly – to give the illusion that it was the crystal that was moving. Then, as though prompted, the crystal actually did start to rotate, seemingly of its own accord. They both watched it, fascinated. 'Look at it: it's going round in circles,' she said.

'Just like me,' he said. 'What does it mean?'

'It means *yes* and *no*.'

'That's a lot of bloody use,' he said. 'Try dowsing the whole of me.'

'Okay: lie on the floor,' she said. I'm just going to get something a bit heavier than this crystal – '

He lay down and watched her as she rummaged around on the mantelpiece. As he lay there, the cat jumped up on his chest again and began nuzzling his chin. 'You might as well do Cleo while you're at it,' he said. 'She ought to be *really* interesting. She's got nine times as many chakras as me.'

She returned and knelt down astride him. Now there was a shiny white bit of rock dangling on the end of the string.

'What's that?' Perkins said.

'A piece of the Temple of Khons,' she said. 'I brought it back from Karnak last year.'

'I thought you were trying to save the environment not wreck it,' he said. 'If everybody was to take a piece of Karnak, there'd be nothing left.'

'Close your eyes and concentrate,' she said, hovering the stone about six inches above his knees, 'or this isn't going to work.'

He pushed the cat away from him and concentrated, but only half-closed his eyes. After a minute or so, she thought she could see something happening: a barely discernible movement...

He squinted down at the stone. It was vibrating without, it seemed, any coaxing from her hand. She let it vibrate for a moment longer then moved it on up to his crotch and suspended it there. He concentrated extra hard, trying to will the pendulum to vibrate even more but it wouldn't respond. She moved it on up to his waist, then on to his heart, where a look of genuine concern came over her face as all movement abruptly stopped. It didn't move at his neck or his eyes either. And when it came to the top of his head, it still hung motionless – immovable as the huge alabaster block from which it had chipped or crumbled.

After several more abortive attempts, she finally stopped trying.

Perkins opened his eyes fully. 'How did I do?' he said. 'What did it say?'

She shook her head, a perplexed look on her face: 'That you haven't got a soul,' she said, matter-of-factly.

'Are you sure?'

'The pendulum never lies,' she said.

'Give it here,' he said, suddenly sitting up. 'There's something wrong with that stone. Which part of Karnak did you pick it up from, anyway? Maybe it's off some sacrificial altar. It's probably riddled with evil spirits.'

'There's nothing wrong with the stone,' she said. 'It's your head that's the problem. You think this is all a big joke. Your trouble is you don't believe in any *thing* or any *body*. That's why the stone won't move for you.'

He stood up. 'Let me try,' he said. 'It must have been the way you were holding it – '

'I've been done already,' she said. 'I know *I've* got a soul.'

He took the stone from her all the same. 'Lie down,' he said, 'and I'll check you out. Best to be sure.'

She lay down on the carpet beside the cat and closed her eyes. He held the stone above her head and steadied it there…

After only a second or two, it started to move – no question about it. He steadied his hand with his other hand but the stone continued to move, the movement becoming a gradual revolution. He moved his hands ever so slightly in a counter-orbit but the stone continued in its course. His wife still had her eyes tightly closed, body stretched out rigid, like a freshly-embalmed Mummy awaiting its twelve hour journey through the Underworld. The stone speeded up. There seemed to be no stopping it. He stared in amazement, semi-hypnotized by the ancient shadow of it carouselling rhythmically over her closed eyes…

'Anything?' she said.

'Not a dickybird,' he said.

That night something woke him in the early hours. He got up and went downstairs. The light was still on in the front room but the little pile of negative objects had gone from the table and the back door was ajar. It was pitch-black outside and there was a light drizzle falling. He stepped out into the yard in his bare feet and tiptoed round to the side of the house. There she was, crouched down by the side of a flower bed, a dark shadow against the fuchsia bush, and he could hear the scrape of a trowel. He watched her for a moment and then went back in and straight to bed. A few minutes later, he listened as the back door closed and she came up the stairs and went into her room. The bed springs twanged as she got in. He waited a long time, until he was sure she was asleep, before getting up and going downstairs again. The trowel was lying on the draining board with wet earth still clinging to it. He picked it up, unbolted the back door and stepped out into the steadily falling rain. At the side of the house, he knelt down in front of the flower bed and started digging…

The Mattress

Perkins didn't dump the mattress over the tip as she'd asked him to, but dumped it over the quarry instead. It was a dark December evening, so nobody saw him. In the time it would have taken to drive to the tip and back, he went and had a pint.

The following morning he went back to have a look. It was a single mattress from the spare bed, anciently torn and stained and they must have slept together on it only about twenty times – when visitors stayed and made love on it perhaps half a dozen times, to the best of his recollection.

It wasn't where he'd left it. Some kids had dragged it from the entrance of the quarry and positioned it on a bend of the new BMX racing track, recently developed by the Council. He stood at the top of the quarry looking down, watching three kids on bikes race each other. None of them would go over the mattress. It lay prostrate, pale blue and vulnerable, soaked through with dew.

Round and round the kids went switch-backing over the three foot high bumps but none of them would go over the mattress. Water cascaded down from a rent in a nearby rock. From where he was he could see the sea and the blur of distant Devon. He needed a pee. Round and round the kids pedalled. He wanted to see if they'd go over the mattress but always at the last moment each one steered away. Then suddenly they were gone, leaving the mattress stretched out pale blue and alone in the vast amphitheatre of the quarry. Their voices tagged along behind, leaving only the sound of falling water.

He walked as far as where the tennis courts had once been, had a pee behind a bush and found the remains of a torn up porno magazine in the long grass nearby. He picked up several faded scraps of what seemed to be a naked man or men and a woman and tried to piece them together but to no avail. When he returned to the quarry some minutes later, the same three boys had come back with three or four of their friends. Round and around they were all going and: one of them must ride over it, he thought but no. Each baulked in his turn. One of them brought hardboard: a thin, torn sheet that he placed over one end of the mattress to bridge the gap. They cycled back to take a run at it: the first one skidded dramatically to a halt inches before the obstacle. Each tried and failed. Bricks and stones were fetched to wedge around the hardboard. One made it up the hardboard ramp but stopped dead in the middle of the mattress. Another did the same and lost his balance, fell. Tyre marks scored the fabric. Then one made it stumblingly; then a second, then a third, each without dismounting. Then the first again, faster. Then it became easy and unremarkable. The mattress was becoming more racing track than mattress. More kids came. A furious traffic of kids and bikes drove over it, laughing and shouting, their voices ricocheting off the quarry walls, vanishing up through cracks and schisms in its sides.

Monkey Business

Halfway through the quarrel, and to reinforce his point, Perkins stormed out. But he didn't feel like going far because it was getting dark and he was hungry and there were two breasts of chicken cooking in the oven: one for him and one for her.

They were what the argument had been about, indirectly. He'd been so hungry when he got home that day, he'd wanted to eat his just as it was but his wife wanted them to sit down together at table for once, with all the trimmings. He should have listened to her and prepared some veg – it wouldn't have taken long – but when you suffered from low blood sugar levels as he did, it wasn't easy to wait.

His wife was sitting in the quiet room when he got back five minutes later. He could see her through the bay window. She had her eyes closed and the light out and was breathing deeply, trying to compose herself. They were like the Spratts as far as blood pressure went: she had to watch her high pressure and he had to watch his low pressure.

When he saw her sitting there totally bereft, he knew he'd come back too soon so, even though by this time he was absolutely ravenous, he went back out again and sat in the park for a further ten minutes.

His wife was watching TV when he got back the second time, and eating a chicken breast, which he later discovered was his. He approached with caution and stood – or rather, 'hovered' – in the gap between kitchen and lounge. He didn't know whether to expect a missile of some sort or a further volley of words but, in the event, she didn't acknowledge his presence in any way and he didn't think she'd even realized he was back. There was a documentary on about people with unusual pets. He stood watching, with his coat still on in case he needed to make a quick getaway. It was an American show. One guy owned a white wolf, which rode behind him everywhere on his motorbike; another owned a cougar which could run at 54 miles an hour and didn't need a motorbike. His cougar wasn't 'wild' he said. Politicians and terrorists were 'wild' compared with his cougar. A man with a chimpanzee came on last of all. It was a very old, perfectly house-trained female. The man thought the world of it. It could understand 500 words of English, could eat at table, smile for the camera and sleep in a normal bed. It liked nothing better than for the man to give it a goodnight kiss and a cuddle before it went to sleep. His voice breaking with emotion, the man said he would do absolutely anything for it. He couldn't imagine life without it. All the girlfriends he'd ever had, had to like it, too. 'Love me, love my monkey,' he said, with a tear in his eye.

Perkins' wife hadn't once turned round while all this was going on and he was convinced she hadn't noticed him. Until, still with her back to him, she said: '*You* want to get one of those.'

The Great Onanist

They were looking at exhibit A: a round, spiral-shaped turd about five inches in diameter, light brown in colour, slightly crusted and pitted with what looked like half-digested peanuts. It had shrunk slightly since Perkins had arrived home from work forty eight hours previous, to find it lying in the middle of a half-ransacked drawer of the Welsh dresser. Since then, it had been confined to the coal-shed, along with the various napkins and tea-towels it had come into contact with. Perkins' wife thought the Agent was unlikely to want to see it but Perkins had brought it in anyway, as further evidence of the trauma they'd undergone.

He thought the Agent would have been hardened to such sights but it was obvious that he'd seen enough. Perkins replaced the sheet of newspaper over the drawer and put it back outside. They could claim for the napkins and tea towels, the Agent said, and he'd also allow them something on the drawer.

Perkins had noticed that he was a man of few words but this last item had clearly unsettled him. He moved quickly on down his list. So far, they'd agreed on nearly everything: the video player, the cassettes, the books, the jewellery. Friends had told them to bump up the list, put in for 'everything bar the kitchen sink' but they were hopeless at deception and this was a genuine claim – but for the two or three minor items Perkins had slipped in at the last minute. In actual fact, he wasn't too upset by the burglary: having financial recompense for all the stuff stolen was like having money in the bank. His wife and he badly needed to get away for a holiday and this had come just at the right time.

Smitten with conscience and cold feet at the last minute, she'd wanted to play it straight down the line but Perkins had told her to let him do the talking. And so far, he'd had to tell only a few half truths: about the clothes, for instance. Mathew had come home the previous week together with a black plastic bag full of laundry. He hadn't told anyone it was laundry but just dumped it by the washing machine next to the bin bags. Perkins wasn't 100% sure whether he or his wife had then dumped it out with the bin bags or whether the burglar had taken it but, for the purposes of the claim, he was giving the burglar the benefit of the doubt. And who was to say if he was wrong? They were never going to catch the bugger anyway.

The Agent carried on down his list and, all the time, Perkins was mentally charting their progress to those golden holiday beaches, basking in the prospect.

But the next item pulled him up sharp: bogus item number 2. 'The binoculars,' the Agent said. 'Can you give me some details on those?' Perkins was just about to, when Mathew came in and, quickly gauging the situation, went upstairs. Perkins started describing the binoculars in great detail – magnification, make, distinguishing features etc. – which was no problem because he'd examined them carefully before hiding them under the bed half an hour before the Agent arrived. The Agent noted it all on his list and was just about to put a tick next to 'Binoculars' when Mathew poked his head over the bannister and shouted down. He was waving something in his hand: 'It's okay – I've found the binoculars, Dad! They were under the bed all the time!'

Perkins rushed upstairs: 'Thank God for that!' he said but when he was out of sight of the Agent, shook his fist at Mathew and mouthed a few murderous oaths. The Agent had already put a line through 'Binoculars' by the time he got back down. 'What a relief!' Perkins said, as though they were some precious family heir loom, instead of just a cheap Car Boot Sale pair. 'I thought I'd seen the last of those.'

They moved further down the list. His wife had guilt written all over her face by now and Perkins guessed he did too, but just a few more items and they'd be home and dry. They deserved that holiday after all the stress they'd been under.

Strangely enough, the next item *was* genuine but Perkins could see the Agent was going to have a problem with it. One of his pictures – an early work from his Neo-Dadaist period – had been part of the haul. He was rather flattered that it had been stolen but his wife had been distinctly peeved that one of her paintings hadn't been burgled as well. He just hoped the picture would end up on a wall and not in some skip.

'This painting you've got down here puzzles me,' the Agent said. 'Who's it by?'

'Me,' Perkins said. 'I'm an artist.'

For the first time, the Agent's expression seemed to soften and he looked quite impressed. 'Do you sell your work?' he said.

'Occasionally,' Perkins said.

'Was this one for sale?'

Perkins hesitated, not quite sure what he was getting at. 'Why I ask,' the Agent continued, 'is because if it was for sale it wouldn't count as a Household Possession. It wouldn't come under your policy.'

'It definitely wasn't for sale,' Perkins told him. 'My wife *loved* that picture.'

The Agent scribbled something down. 'You've put down £200 as the value,' he said. 'I'm not sure how we're going to validate that figure. Are you well-known?'

'Very,' Perkins lied. 'I've had exhibitions all over the place. My work's been reviewed. It's much sought-after. I'm probably the most burglarable artist in South Wales.'

Levity was a big mistake. 'But I've never heard of you,' the Agent said.

'That's not surprising,' Perkins said. 'My markets are mostly in London, Paris and New York.'

The Agent looked impressed again. 'If we decide to pay out, I'll need a description and a price,' he said. 'A description first – ' He stood there, pen poised. Perkins wasn't sure where to begin. 'It's a collage,' his wife put in – her first words since the Agent had arrived. He started writing. 'More *mixed media*,' Perkins corrected. The Agent scored through 'collage'. 'But there's a lot of collage in it,' Perkins added.

'What's it called?' the Agent asked.

'The Great Onanist,' Perkins told him.

'The Great *what?*'

'O-NA-NIST,' Perkins said. 'The Great Onanist.'

The Agent wrote it down but it was obvious he hadn't a clue what it meant. As he was writing, Perkins' wife excused herself and went out in the kitchen, guessing that Perkins was about to launch into a description. That was going to be difficult to accomplish without giving the impression that she was married to some kind of pervert. Perkins began by describing the picture's artistic lineage, asked if the Agent had heard of Dali or Dada or the Surrealists. He hadn't. 'Well Dali did this big painting called *The Great Masturbator*,' Perkins told him, 'and I got the idea from that. Of course, my picture's totally different in concept and execution but – ' The Agent cut him short, asked if he'd got a photo of it. Perkins hadn't, but 'D'you know 'The Hay Wain' by Constable?' he asked. The Agent's eyes lit up. Not only did he know it but he owned a set of Constables: six place mats with a Constable on each one. He was pretty sure 'The Hay Wain' was among them. It was a small world!

'Well, I've taken a print – an ordinary, common-or-garden print, of 'The Hay Wain' by Constable,' Perkins said, 'and superimposed a photographic image on top of it.'

The Agent looked confused. 'Of what?' he said.

'Of a man,' Perkins told him. 'Of a naked man who once worked in the Folies Bergère in Paris. He was a contortionist. He could bend his body into all sorts of shapes. In the picture I've used, he's sitting down with his head tucked between his legs so that it looks as though he's engaged in an act of' – Perkins lowered his voice an octave – '*self-abuse.*'

Now the Agent looked embarrassed as well as confused. 'You stuck that on 'The Hay Wain'?' he said. 'Where?'

'As a matter of fact, right over 'The Hay Wain' itself,' Perkins told him.

He could see the next question forming even before it left the Agent's lips: '*Why?*' he said.

Perkins wished he hadn't asked. Now a lengthy exposition, quoting various precursors, was called for, and he didn't have the time or the inclination. He tried to sum up: 'It's a surreal statement, pure and simple,' he said. 'Like the meeting of an umbrella and a sewing machine on an operating table – ' The Agent looked at Perkins as though he was the one who should be on the operating table. He seemed about to say something but shook his head and went on writing.

At that moment, Perkins' wife came back in from the kitchen and asked if they wanted a cup of tea. The Agent declined. He'd been sidetracked enough already. He obviously wanted to get out of there, there and then – home to some sanity: watercolours of Gower beaches, tea and crumpets off Constable's Hay Wain. He looked at his list again and couldn't conceal his relief: the very last item.

'One pair of men's spectacles?' he said.

'That's right,' Perkins said.

'Why would they want to steal your glasses?'

'They didn't steal them,' Perkins said. 'They broke them.'

'Why would they want to break them?' the Agent said.

'Who knows,' Perkins said. 'Just plain vandalism, I suppose.'

The Agent shook his head. He seemed more astonished by this than the turd in the drawer.

'They actually *broke* your glasses?' he said, still trying to take it in. 'Can I see them?'

For the first time, Perkins was caught completely off guard. He hadn't planned on having to actually produce the glasses. He'd thought it was such an insignificant item that the Agent would just accept his word. His wife's new-found calm dissolved into barely suppressed panic. 'Certainly,' he said. 'I'll just nip upstairs and fetch them – ' He ran upstairs to the bedroom, to be confronted by Mathew, with a knowing grin on his face, waiting with the glasses. He'd just taken them from the bedside table, where Perkins had placed them the previous night, just before he'd closed his book and switched off the light. Perkins took them from him with another murderous glare. They were only three months old and in perfectly good, A1, working order but, nevertheless, after only a momentary hesitation, he snapped them in half. And somehow, when he'd done it, that didn't seem enough – not sufficiently convincing – so he broke off the wing pieces and snapped them in half, too. The

Agent was still waiting. He could hear his wife talking to him, nervously discussing the weather or the soaring crime rate, perhaps. He now had six pieces in his hand but they needed a final touch: a coup-de-grâce of some sort. He looked around for something to break the lenses with but Mathew was already one step ahead. He'd spotted an old cricket bat on top of the wardrobe, which he handed to Perkins with obvious delight. Perkins held the glasses on the bed – to deaden the sound – and struck the lenses two swift blows. Now there were more than a dozen pieces and he realized – too late – that this was overkill. He ran back downstairs, out of breath and panting. When he held out his hand to reveal the telltale evidence, his wife had gone bright red for him. The Agent studied the pieces with patent incredulity. Perkins sensed that, in all his years as an Insurance Agent, he had never come across anything like this before. This put the turd well and truly in the shade. Then, for one horrible moment, it looked as though he might not swallow it after all, that the game might suddenly be up. But, instead, he shook his head wearily as though despairing of the whole human race: 'Good God!' he said, 'What kind of a *maniac* would do a thing like that!'

Culture

For some reason, Perkins' wife didn't want him to go out that particular night but it was a Tuesday night and Tuesday night, as she well knew, was Pool Night. Couldn't he break the routine just for once, she asked? O.D. wouldn't mind. In all the years they'd been playing, Perkins had never let him down, so what difference could one night make? It wasn't asking too much. They could open a bottle of wine and have a cosy night together by the fire, listening to some good music: something they hadn't done for ages.

It was tempting but, what she didn't seem to realize – and what Perkins couldn't seem to get through to her – was that O.D. and he had always played on a Tuesday night. From time immemorial. Asking him to suddenly change his routine was like asking a plain ball to change into stripes.

So Perkins made her a cup of tea and a sandwich, lit the fire and left her watching Eastenders. But, as it happened, he may as well have stayed home. He had a disastrous night on the table. He couldn't understand why, but the balls just weren't running for him. They hadn't been all day.

After the game, he persuaded O.D. to go for a pint in the Ty Tawe Arts Centre. An old friend of his was the Guest reader there, supported by readers from the Llewlas Writers' Circle. It was further to go than their usual pub but Perkins thought it would make a nice change and O.D. needn't worry: the reading would probably be over by the time they got there.

And that was where he snookered himself yet again. When they got there, the reading was in full swing and not in the Lecture Theatre – which had proved too big for the moderate-sized audience – but in the Bar itself. Consequently, before Perkins could stop him, O.D. took off like a bat out of hell. And Perkins would have followed suit but was gambling on the reading being just about at an end. He waited for the applause between readers and went in. There were no seats left, so he squeezed his way through to the back of the Bar and leaned on the counter. The counter flap was up but there was no sign of the barman. The next reader got up: 'One of the oldest and most respected members of the Llewlas Writers' Circle,' the chairman announced, '…has been published in Nib, Stanza and the letters column of the *South Wales Evening Echo…*'

There was an enthusiastic round of applause and several impromptu shouts of encouragement. Perkins spotted the barman then. He was sitting down in the audience, which seemed to comprise of most of the Llewlas Writers' Circle and their supporters. He spotted his friend Iuean, too, sitting out the front, looking thoroughly pissed off. He hadn't noticed him before because his head was buried in his hands. Perkins knew the feeling. Iuean's half of the programme had finished long ago and he just wanted to collect his cheque and go.

How many readers had there been and how many more *were* there, Perkins wondered? Everybody had a drink in front of them, except him: a drink and a slim sheaf of poems. When the oldest and most respected member of the Llewlas Writers' Circle had finished his set and sat down, the barman got up – not to attend to the Bar but to read his own poems. Perkins looked at his watch: it was ten fifteen. He'd give it another half hour and then he was going – no matter how ignorant it looked. Even if Ted Hughes, Seamus Heaney and Pablo Neruda all stepped up to the lectern together, he was still only giving it half an hour.

The barman returned to his seat amid rapturous applause and, after a bit, Perkins actually started listening to the poetry. He couldn't decide whether losing heavily on the baize or his lack of a drink was affecting his critical faculties, but it seemed like some of the worst he'd ever heard. And what amazed him, far more than the awfulness of it, was the supreme confidence of the readers. And the more confident they were, the more awful were the poems. A couple of them even had the audacity to write about the terrible pain of being a poet.

Perkins couldn't understand it, because he knew Llewlas well. It was a rough, tough but salt-of-the-earth, solidly Working Class area of Town, currently battling a huge drugs problem. He'd worked there for thirteen years and there was a time, well within his memory, when the average resident's idea of recreation was the Bingo Hall, the Cinema, the Pub or the Club. What had gone wrong he asked himself. Why this sudden, inexplicable urge to be poets? They *all* seemed to be at it.

The Arts Council must shoulder some of the blame, he concluded. Instead of providing financial support, they ought to have been setting up Betty Ford-type clinics before some of these would-be writers were too far gone. From the evidence of what he'd heard so far, Perkins couldn't help concluding that literary aspirations in the wrong hands were more dangerous than crack, heroin and LSD all put together. They were obviously contagious in Llewlas and ought to be stamped out before they reached epidemic proportions.

When he eventually got out of there, about twenty poems later, not a drop of drink had passed his lips and he hadn't even had a chance to speak to Ieuan. Between the poetry and the Pool and the lack of alcohol, he walked home in a state of deep depression.

His wife was kneeling on the floor, listening to Classic FM, when he got back. Her last words to him before he'd gone out had been: 'Don't drink too much,' so he stood there, steady as a rock, eager to show her how sober he was. But she didn't look up. The floor around her was strewn with still-wet paintings and there was a peculiar smell of burning in the air. Perkins sniffed a couple of times but it wasn't the stove or the oven or the fire, which had long-since gone out. His wife had been busy. She was wearing an old painting shirt and there was paint on her hands and in her hair. The paintings were wild and whorling abstracts and the music on the ghetto-blaster was loud and soul-stirringly familiar: *'Rachmaninov's Third Piano Concerto!'* Perkins said, with perfect enunciation. 'With Alfred Brendel on piano, if I'm not mistaken.'

He knew, as he said it, it was a mistake but he wanted to prove he was still articulate and in full control of his faculties. She groaned and shook her head. 'Must you *always* do that?' she said.

'Do what?' Perkins said.

'Give me the title and composer of every bit of music that ever comes on.'

'Do I?' he said.

'Yes you do,' she said. 'Can't you just listen and enjoy it for what it is without this constant compulsion to show off your superior knowledge? It makes me sick. I can't watch a film or a play without you giving me the complete cast list, right down to the Assistant Gaffer and Tea-boy. Why do you have to do it all the time? Were you like that when you were a kid: always showing off?'

Perkins had never said boo to a goose when he was a kid, but she didn't give him a chance to say so. 'I can just see you and your family sitting round the radio listening to music,' she went on: '"That's *Rachmaninov's Third Piano Concerto*, Mummy!" "No, it isn't, son: that's *Beethoven*." "I'm sure you're both wrong, my dear: it's definitely *Mozart*." For Christ's sake, just enjoy the music for what it *is*!'

It was just a hunch before, but Perkins now got the distinct impression that she wasn't glad to see him. 'Sorry, love,' he said. 'You're quite right: I'm always doing that. It won't happen again.'

His placatory tone threw her. 'Are you drunk?' she said, looking at him for the first time.

'I wish I was,' Perkins said. 'What's that smell?'

'Sage,' she said. 'I've been smudging.'

'Smudging? What's that?' Perkins said, imagining it was some new graphic technique she'd developed while he'd been out.

But it was nothing to do with Art. 'It's something the Native Americans used to do,' she said. 'They used to burn sage in every room. They reckoned it cleared the air – cleaned out all the bad energy. I lit some just after you went out tonight.'

'Smells like herbal cigarettes,' Perkins said. 'How does it work? Do you go around smudging the ash on everything?'

'No, it's just the smoke,' she said. 'You burn it in something and carry it round from room to room. It clears away all the negative energy.'

'I could have done with some sage tonight,' he said and started to tell her about the reading but she hated readings even more than O.D. did and cut him short in mid-sentence. 'What about the paintings?' she said. 'You haven't said anything about the paintings. Am I improving?'

He looked at them more closely – from all angles – but couldn't make anything out. She hadn't painted for ages and they weren't like her usual stuff. These were wilder and more abstract. She'd used up a hell of a lot of paint on them. All of it applied in an apparent frenzy.

Then he said what he always said about her work when he was momentarily in two minds: *'Brilliant!'*

She looked quietly relieved. 'And you can tell what I'm trying to say?'

'Of course.'

'What?'

He hesitated.

The truth dawned on her: 'You don't really like them, do you?' she said.

'Of course I do,' he said. 'But don't start getting too intellectual, that's all. It'll kill everything.'

'What d'you mean *"intellectual"?'* she said. *'You're* the Intellectual.'

He could tell he was getting out of his depth. He didn't know why he'd said "intellectual". Maybe because of the lack of anything immediately recognizable in the work. 'What I mean is,' he said, picking his way across this sudden minefield, 'paint what you *feel* not what you *think* you should feel. Don't force the imagery.' She looked at him searchingly. He knew that look. There was very bad energy welling up behind it. 'Are you *sure* you haven't been drinking?' she said.

'God's honour,' he said. But she wasn't convinced. She got up from the floor and advanced on him: 'Let me smell your breath – '

He backed away instinctively – although he had absolutely nothing to hide – and as he did so, something stuck to his foot. He tried to kick it off before she noticed but it stayed stuck. And then, when she was almost upon him, as though by divine providence, a familiar chord struck up on the radio. He should have ignored it but **'Schumann's First Piano Concerto!'** he blurted out, before he could stop himself.

That was definitely the last straw. She went to bed not long after that, convinced he was drunk and not worth talking to. There was no point in him denying it or saying sorry or trying to convince her that he actually liked her work a lot and thought she had a unique talent.

When he was sure she was gone, he peeled the picture off his shoe and tried to touch it up, using some of the paint she'd left out but, try as he might, he couldn't recapture the violence and verve of her brush-strokes.

Later, he wandered around from room to room and, sure enough, there was a smell of burning sage in each of them. It smelt particularly strong in his study. He cleaned his teeth, crossed the landing, undressed, got into bed, put out the light and closed his eyes – all to the smell of burning sage. He went to sleep and the smell of burning sage followed him into his wildest dreams. At one point, he found himself in a vast, moonlit, Death Valley of a desert full of burning sage-brush. He was dying of thirst and on his last legs but scattered all around were mirage-like members of the Llewlas Writers' Circle, buried to their necks in the sand, their heads swarming with termites – every man-Jack of them script-less and half-blind – but still relentlessly mouthing their lines to the star-spangled Milky Way…

Friends, Romans and Countrymen

1

It was blowing a gale outside but Perkins had just lit the fire and put the kettle on and shoved two lamb chops in the oven. It had been a bad day. A radiator had unexpectedly fallen off the wall that morning and flooded half the front room. Perkins had eventually found the stopcock and turned it off but it would be the next day, at least, before the plumber could get the heating going again.

Perkins had mopped up most of the mess but he didn't know what his wife was going to say when she got back. She'd gone on one of her Self-Healing weekends again but the sight of her ruined carpet was going to give her a relapse. She'd been on about the loose radiator for years but it was too late to cry over spilt radiator water now. For the moment, the fire was blazing nicely – casting a warm reassuring glow on the walls – the TV was on and there was a smell of sizzling chops wafting across at him from the kitchen. Suddenly, the world didn't seem so cruel after all.

He'd just about got his mouth ready for the chops when there was a tap on the window. He got up and peeped through the Venetian blinds and there was a pair of haunted-looking eyes staring back at him, which he recognized almost immediately as Jimmy's.

He let him in out of the rain. Jimmy was an old friend of theirs: the three of them – Perkins, his wife and Jimmy – had been through College together, graduated, married and had kids round about the same time. Jimmy had been the life and soul of the College and one of its brightest talents but the traumas of his current divorce were putting a severe strain on his friends. Perkins and his wife had been getting almost weekly instalments of the unfolding saga for months.

Jimmy made his usual chirpy entrance, took off his coat and bee-lined straight for the fireplace, where he crouched with his back to Perkins, warming his hands. 'Where's Liz?' he said, as Perkins poured him a mug of tea. When he learnt of her Self-Healing course his disappointment was patent. They all seemed to come to Perkins' wife when they needed a shoulder to cry on but, for once, he was going to have to make do with Perkins. Perkins handed him the mug. Jimmy obviously couldn't wait to tell him about the court case but, Perkins made a pre-emptive strike by telling him about the radiator first. His words just seemed to pass over Jimmy's head. He sat down in an arm chair, lit a cigarette and inhaled deeply: *'Sixty thousand pounds,'* he said staring into the fireplace. 'That's what the judge awarded her. *Sixty thousand pounds* – and six weeks to pay.'

Perkins switched off the TV. *Sixty thousand pounds!* He didn't know what to say. He knew she'd asked for eighty: so was sixty good or bad? He tried to give a considered opinion but Jimmy wasn't interested in what Perkins thought. He just wanted to think aloud, and for the next three hours that was all he did: think aloud. Talk and talk. And Perkins listened and didn't listen as, yet again, Jimmy was transmogrified into the various characters in a one-man Greek Tragedy: his wife, his kids, her parents, his best friend, his doctor, his bank manager, his solicitor and now the Barrister and Judge as well. Perkins felt as though he knew them all personally: the tyrannical father, the emotionless mother, the snooty sister, the sympathetic doctor, the mercenary legal aides. He even knew some of their more caustic marriage lines by heart: *"I **never** loved you"… "You stole my **youth**"… "The **kids** don't love you either…You were **never** a father to them."*

And throughout it all, Jimmy asked the same questions he'd asked a thousand times before: Where did he go wrong? Should he have married a girl half his age? Should he have given her three kids in four years? Was it Acute Post-Natal Depression or did she *really* hate him? And all the time this soul-searching was going on, Perkins was thinking of the chops in the oven: should he have put them on the timer? Were they or weren't they done? Would they have caramelised by now? Should he turn them up or down? Every time he heard a car pull up, he thought it was his wife. But there was no escape. He kept making mug after mug of tea, checking on the chops, stoking the fire, wondering where in the wild and blustery world his wife was and why she wasn't there, taking her share of all that misery. He got so desperate, he went out in the hallway and rang several times to see if his wife had left the Self-Healing Centre but the line was always engaged. Jimmy carried on talking each time he went to phone but then, as abruptly as he'd arrived, he had his coat on ready to leave. Perkins found himself telling him not to go just yet if he didn't want to, but he couldn't be dissuaded. He thanked Perkins for listening but before he went, there was one last favour he wanted to ask. Could he draw one of Liz's Medicine Cards?

Perkins went and fetched them. Whenever Jimmy called, it was a ritual for him to pick a card before he went, to help him on his way. This time he picked *The Bat*. Perkins read out the caption. If he wanted to advance in life, it said, he needed to open his ears and listen more to other people. Jimmy was astounded by this insight and so was Perkins. 'That's spot on, isn't it?' Jimmy said. 'Most of the time I don't *listen*. That's half my problem: I talk but I don't *listen*. Jan was always telling me that – but I just wouldn't *listen*.'

The gale was still blowing outside. At the front door, Jimmy gave Perkins a hug. 'Look at it this way,' Perkins said, offering consolation and hope, 'It's nearly all over now. Soon you'll be footloose and fancy free!'

Jimmy pulled up his collar and ducked into the rain. 'Foot-loose and **fifty-three!**' he called back, as the grim night swallowed him up.

Perkins could smell the smoke almost as soon as he shut the door. He rushed to the oven: the chops had caramelised alright and so had half the oven. He tipped the two cremated lumps into the bin, opened all doors and windows and stood in the middle of the room wind-milling two tea towels. The last of the smoke was just billowing away into the darkness when his wife came in. He didn't like the look of her. She didn't notice the smoke or the carpet or the radiator but flopped down in the same armchair that Jimmy had just vacated. She looked washed out, so Perkins played down the disasters of the previous twenty-four hours, made them sound trivial, farcical even. But she didn't laugh and, in fact, made no comment whatsoever. Perkins stoked the fire and made her a cup of tea. They sat watching TV in unnatural silence for half an hour and, at first he was glad of the peace and quiet but, after a bit, the atmosphere started to get to him and he just had to say what was on his mind: 'Are you sure these courses are doing you any good?' he said, 'because every time you come back from them, you seem upset.'

'I'm fine,' she said.

'Only, I've read somewhere that group therapy can get out of hand,' Perkins said. 'Unless you know what you're doing.'

'It's alright,' she said. 'It's just that I've got to learn to face myself. Confront all the shit in my life. Come to terms with it.'

'What shit?' Perkins said, half-expecting her to include *him* under that heading.

'All the shit of my past and present lives,' she said. 'All the things that have stayed hidden for years. I need to open doors.'

'It's okay to open doors,' Perkins said, 'as long as you know what to do once they're open. If you don't, it's better to leave them closed. All this soul-searching can tie you in knots. Jimmy's always trying to open doors and look at the mess he's in.'

'But at least he's trying to confront where he went wrong – to understand what needs to be put right,' she said. 'The healing process is a painful one but he'll get there in the end.'

'I don't know so much,' Perkins said. 'Jimmy confronted himself for *three* hours tonight in that very chair. He was tormented coming in and he was tormented going out. Nothing he said or did or confronted in between, made a blind bit of difference.'

'You don't understand,' she said. 'You've never tried to confront yourself. Everybody needs to know themselves.'

Perkins didn't want to press the point any more and was sorry he'd made it in the first place. He'd had enough of human suffering for one day. At that precise point in time, he didn't want to confront himself or anyone else, for that matter. It was late and all he wanted to do was get to bed.

The fire had burnt to ashes when they finally got there. The wind and the rain had died down by the early hours and it was then that he could hear her crying, sobbing quietly into the pillow next to him. At first, he wondered if she could be crying over him: over something he'd said or done, over the radiator or the carpet or all that mysterious *shit* she'd mentioned. Was it something recent or long-standing? He couldn't imagine so, in the end, he rolled over to face her. 'What is it?' he said. 'What's the matter?'

She wouldn't tell him at first and then she said, 'Nothing you can do anything about. And you wouldn't understand if I told you. It's just something that came up this weekend – something I thought I'd forgotten about for good – and when I suddenly remembered, I couldn't stop crying. I felt such a fool – in front of everybody. It was so silly.'

'What was it?' Perkins said. 'What did you remember?'

Her breath was coming in little uncontrollable shudders. He put his hand out and could feel the wet of her tears. 'I remembered Bonzo,' she said.

'Bonzo?' Perkins said, withdrawing his hand. 'Who's Bonzo?'

'My dog,' she said. 'When I was small I had this dog called Bonzo. He was a lovely dog. I always thought of him as human. He was like a brother to me. I loved him more than I loved my parents. And when they asked us at one of these sessions to delve back into our childhood – the first person I saw was Bonzo. He was the first living thing I ever felt close to. I was devastated when he was killed.'

'How did it happen?' Perkins said.

Her voice struggled against a surge of emotion. 'I think it was suicide,' she said. 'He was old and ill. Looking back, I suppose he didn't want to be a burden on anyone, so he just wandered away one day and lay down with his head on the railway lines. My parents had other dogs after that but never one I loved as much as Bonzo. He was special.'

Perkins lay there, holding her hand now, trying to chose the right words to say, but there didn't seem to be any. When he was a kid, his family had got through a dog, three cats, a parrot, a tortoise and innumerable goldfish, so he knew how she felt. He'd written a poem when the dog died and made little wooden crosses for each of the cats but he hadn't cried over them in a long, long time. He didn't tell her any of that, though. He just held her hand in the dark and they both lay there thinking of Bonzo...

2

Perkins was luckier the next time Jimmy called round. His wife was downstairs watching her favourite Soap and he was upstairs in the bedroom reading a book. He heard a knock at the front door and his wife answering it and sounding pleasantly surprised.

Jimmy sounded full of beans, although Perkins knew it was just a front and wouldn't last long once he got going. He could hear them go in the front room and Jimmy asking after him and his wife saying that he was upstairs having a lie down and would probably be down in a minute. As soon as he heard that, he rolled off the bed, tiptoed across the landing and stood at the top of the stairs, listening. The TV had been turned down and Jimmy was already in full spate. It was the usual saga but didn't sound half as dispiriting hearing it from up there as in the actual room.

Perkins went back in the bedroom after a bit and tried to read his book but could still hear Jimmy's voice. His wife didn't seem to be getting a word in edgeways. Ages went by. Perkins began to feel guilty about hiding away. Jimmy had always been, and always would be, a true and valued friend but Perkins just couldn't bear his pain any more. It was dragging him under. He stuck it out for a while longer and then felt he just had to go down. It wasn't an entirely altruistic move. There was half a bottle of whisky in the Welsh dresser that he badly needed to get his hands on.

Neither of them paid any attention to Perkins when he walked in: they were far too wrapped up in Jimmy's problems. Perkins said hello and went straight to the Welsh dresser, which was in the adjoining kitchenette. He got three glasses and started to pour the whisky. As he did so, he could hear Jimmy telling her what an amazing mishap he'd had since his last visit. The Tarot card he'd drawn then, had specifically told him he needed to 'listen more' and when he'd got home he'd gone and put Superglue in his ear by mistake. Somehow a tube of Superglue had found its way into the medicine cabinet next to his ear ointment. He'd had to go down the hospital. They said it would work its own way out in time and that they wouldn't risk scraping it out in case the eardrum came with it. So he was temporarily deaf in that ear. It was full of Locktite. But how ironic, he said, that that should have happened straight after he'd drawn the Tarot card.

Perkins poured them three big ones, drank his and poured himself another.

'Apparently, there's only one other person in the whole of Britain has ever done that before,' Jimmy was saying, when Perkins took the drinks into them. 'A man from Wigan. I almost made medical history – '

Perkins' wife thought it was all very strange and significant but Perkins thought he should have been more careful where he stored the Locktite. Jimmy was such a bad listener, Perkins doubted if he'd ever *had* eardrums but he light-heartedly suggested that if the eardrum were to come out by mistake, it would be a good opportunity to sand it down and pop it back in again or, if the worst came to the worst, he might try sandblasting the Locktite out by way of his other ear.

His wife told him to be serious. How would he like Locktite in *his* ear?' At that particular moment, with Jimmy gearing up for an all-night session on the agony couch, Perkins wouldn't have minded a bit.

Perkins sat down on the end of the settee and hugged his glass and tried to look serious, while Jimmy started giving an inventory of everything he'd had to hand over in the divorce settlement. The list hadn't changed since the last time: sixty grand, the kids and nearly everything else bar the kitchen sink – except that she'd forgotten to claim the ironing board, a fact which seemed to give him immense satisfaction. 'She got the iron but not the ironing board. She forgot to put it down on the list. So that stays.'

As usual, Perkins' wife was a model of sympathy and compassion. If Jimmy's abiding problem was that he never listened, Perkins' wife's was that she listened too much. She had a shoulder ever-ready to be cried on by all and sundry.

Jimmy was a particular challenge for her, though, and she seemed determined to leave no stone of his tortured psyche unturned. She was trying to open doors for him that he had no idea existed – and he was wallowing in the attention. She got him talking about his first meeting with Jan. What had they seen in each other? How did their love first blossom? There might be some clues there about what went wrong later. Jimmy held nothing back. He laid it all on them: courtship, marriage, parenthood, estrangement and eventual breakdown of all communication.

Perkins had stopped making jokes by this point, but he had blotted his copybook and every time he tried to make a constructive comment, they talked over him as though he wasn't there. He sat glumly listening, not speaking unless he was spoken to, which was hardly at all.

Jimmy's fundamental problem seemed to be in deciding whether his wife was ill, insane or genuinely didn't love him any more. And, on balance, he seemed to prefer the second option.

Inevitably, the conversation took an astrological turn – as Perkins knew it must. Jimmy thought he could see the root of all his troubles in their Chinese birth signs: he was a Snake, Jan was a Rat, her mother was a Rabbit and her father was a Rooster. Roosters couldn't show their feelings. Rabbits were all for the quiet life as long as they got their own way. Rats were impulsive go-getters who had to have everything there and then and Snakes had it all but worried over nothing. Perkins' wife was a Rabbit too, as it turned out and Perkins was a Horse: highly-strung and emotional with a tendency to lose friends due to his impatience. Between them, they made quite a menagerie.

Perkins went and poured himself another one and when he came back the conversation had shifted from the astrological to the metaphysical plain: 'She's angry at *herself*,' his wife was saying. 'She didn't see *you* as *you*. She saw *you* as all the things her father *wasn't*.'

Jimmy couldn't have agreed more: 'She saw *me* as a reflection of *her*. But I am *me* and she is *her*.'

'Forget *her*, Jimmy. Think of *you*. Get in touch with *yourself*.'

'I could be like *her*. But if I can understand *me*, I've got it made.'

'Be content with the moment of your *own* being. Face life for what it *is* – '

'It's nihilistic. I have to face that. I have to face the emptiness of my own being…'

Perkins needed to face the emptiness of his own glass: he went and poured more whiskies: one each for them and three for himself.

'You've got to distance yourself, Jimmy,' his wife was saying, when he returned. 'Look at yourself in the mirror. You're all tensed up. You need to relax.'

Jimmy got up and looked at himself in the mirror. 'You're right,' he said. 'Look at me: I'm all tensed up – '

'Your energy isn't going anywhere. It's draining away. You need to go away for a break. Take a holiday. You owe it to yourself.'

This was the first sensible thing Perkins had heard her say all night. If they could only get him away to sunnier climes – Greece or Spain or *anywhere* – it would give them all a break, time to recover. They owed it to themselves. He took some travel brochures down off the bookshelf and started flicking through them: 'Kos looks nice,' he said, 'or how about Crete?' But he was talking to himself again.

Jimmy sat down and the self-questioning began anew: had her strict Catholic upbringing had something to do with it? Was that why his marriage had seemed more like an Inquisition than a marriage? Was he too old for her? Why was she turning the kids against him? Why did her parents hate him? Did she *really* hate him or was it an *'imbalance in the hormones'*? Was she in love with her father or had her father been in love with *her* all the time?

Perkins turned the pages. The whisky was definitely hitting the spot but he still needed to distance himself. 'Or how about an 18 to 25 year-old holiday in Ibiza?' he put in. 'Lots of lovely unattached girls – '

He might as well have been invisible. 'It'll be a release for you when she vacates the premises,' his wife went on. 'But it'll be painful: like a bereavement. There'll be a lot of grief and it's going to take a lot of coming to terms with, Jimmy – but do what I always do when I'm under stress: put a big "S" on your forehead. "S" for SURVIVAL.'

Perkins had put a big "S" on his own forehead as soon as he'd heard Jimmy downstairs, but it didn't seem to be working. He replaced the brochures, went back out the kitchen and poured himself the last of the whisky. In his own quiet way, he felt he was gradually getting to know himself.

'You need someone to make sense of your life, Jimmy,' his wife was saying, as he flopped back down. 'My friend Geena does massage. You should let her get to work on your meridians. Half an hour with her and you won't know yourself. I was all tensed up like you but she taught me to listen to my body and do something about it. Silence is important as well as listening. The Native Americans grew up in silence. For the first six or seven years of their lives they hardly said a word, they just listened. And that's what you've got to do, Jimmy: listen to what your body's telling you. It wasn't a mistake that you put that glue in your ear.'

'What d'you mean?' Jimmy said. 'You think *she* had something to do with it?'

'No, of course not,' she said. 'What I mean is, you put it in because your body was trying to tell you something. It was a subliminal act. You were punishing yourself. And now you need to realign yourself. To slow down. You've got so much anger inside yourself. You've got to get rid of it somehow.'

'You're right,' Jimmy said. 'I can see it all now: the Locktite was symptomatic. It's the end of the marriage so why should I have to listen to her now? I need to listen to my own body more. She's Pisces anyway. *And* she's a Rat.'

'You see,' she said, 'those tarot cards are like your dreams. They tell you things.'

'Funny you should say that,' Jimmy said. 'I haven't dreamt for ages but the other night I dreamt about Pablo Prys. Remember Pablo? We met on the cliff path to Rhosili. It was a beautiful day and I hadn't seen him since the old Art College days, thirty years or more ago. He hadn't changed a bit. Still the same old Pablo. He had an easel under one arm and a canvas under the other. We stood there talking for ages.

'What did he say?' she said.

Jimmy looked blank: 'I can't remember.'

'Try,' she said. 'It's important. It could be a message. We can change the course of our dreams if we want to and learn from them. Pablo may have been trying to tell you something. Think, Jimmy. *Think*.'

Jimmy tried hard to cast his mind back. 'Pablo' Prys had been the enfant terrible of the Painting Department and the bane of the lecturers' lives. He was one of Perkins' early mentors – as far as drinking went, at least – and a guiding light in his formative years. Perkins sat there, cosily sipping the last of the whisky, as Jimmy racked his brains trying to think. It was painful to watch him. But it was all too much: he shook his head and gave up. 'No, it's no good,' he said. 'It's *gone*. I know he was telling me something really important – but I just wasn't listening…'

Perkins didn't see Jimmy pick a card that night – he'd blacked out on the settee long before he'd left – but he hoped he'd have better luck with it than the previous one he'd drawn.

His wife was washing the glasses at the sink when he woke up. He got up unsteadily and tried to put his arms around her. She looked exhausted – even more of a nervous wreck than Jimmy. 'Did you *have* to drink so much?' she said, dropping an empty bottle in the bin. 'That was half-full yesterday.'

Perkins felt only faint remorse. 'I *had* too,' he said. 'How else could I have sat through all that? It was sheer hell.'

'I know it was,' she said, 'but it was important for him to get it all out of his system. To have someone lend a sympathetic ear.'

'One without Locktite in?' Perkins said.

'He just wanted a few answers, that's all,' she said, 'and all you could do was make jokes.'

'I was just trying to cheer him up,' Perkins said, ' – to take his mind off things.'

'He needed help not wisecracks. You were way out of order – '

Perkins slumped back down on the settee again. He knew that wasn't entirely fair – and so did she. He was about to remind her how much he actually liked and admired Jimmy – always had done – and was genuinely concerned about him; that he *had* been trying to help and had a lot of positive things he might have contributed to the conversation – if only they'd given him the chance. But it was past midnight and his hangover was just beginning to kick in. And what was the point in telling her all that, anyway? He knew she wouldn't listen.

The Tunisian Open, '97

The pool table was early Carthaginian, the surface made of some sort of coarse plastic, over which the balls skidded and rolled with a will of their own. It was partitioned off by some potted plants from the rest of the ballroom area where even now, at mid-afternoon, a score of elderly couples were dancing to some Forties Big Band music. The recreation area looked directly out onto the patio, which was dotted with only a sprinkling of sunbathers but Perkins was still surprised to see so many people up and about. The El Hammammet seemed to cater mainly for retired English and German couples, who ought to have been more in need of a siesta at that hour than a waltz or a fox-trot.

It was $90°+$ in the shade outside and warm inside, even with the air-conditioning. While his brother-in-law went to the bar for refills, Perkins sat down on the bench and took the opportunity to 'doctor' Ray's tip with a mixture of beer and cigarette ash. It was the penultimate day of their holiday and, overall, Perkins was now ten or twelve frames down for the series, in what he and Ray had jokingly dubbed 'The Tunisian Open.' They were the only two contestants and the tournament had been as much a test of their cheating skills as their potting ones. Though both were equally adept at the former, luck and the state of the table definitely seemed to be working in Ray's favour. On top of which Ray, being stone-deaf, was impervious to the blare of the loudspeakers.

He returned with the drinks, set them down on the bench and slid some change into the slot for the next frame. As Perkins broke off, he noticed a German couple approaching on their way to the patio. They both wore sunglasses and the man was sweating profusely from his exertions on the dance floor. When they drew level, the man paused to smile at Perkins and Ray and place a coin on the edge of the table. He pointed towards the patio and said something to them in halting English, from which they deduced that he wanted to play the winner.

Ray took up his cue, unaware that it had been tampered with and, to Perkins' amazement, potted his first shot and snookered him with his second.

The Tunisian DJ had begun interspersing the Big Band numbers with popular Forces' Favourites: *Lili Marlene, Run Rabbit Run, Hang Out Your Washing on the Siegfried Line* and many of the dancers were joining in singing, as well as dancing, to the lyrics.

Perkins fluked himself out of trouble and pulled the game back to level pegging but as Ray lined up on yet another frame-clinching shot, desperate measures were called for. He ducked abruptly into Ray's line of vision, waving a hand to get his attention. 'Car-thage!' he mouthed, slowly and deliberately: 'To-morr-ow we go to Car-thage!'

Ray faltered, one eye on Perkins' lips the other on the pot. When the penny dropped, he rose to the bait, puffing out his cheeks in exasperation: if there was one thing he hated more than anything else, it was Culture. Market, beach or pool – yes, but definitely not ruins. 'Car-thage? No way! Waste of time – and money !'

'Ve-ry fam-ous place,' Perkins persisted, 'Hann-i-bal born there –'

Ray shook his head again – vigorously. He'd had enough of museums and ancient monuments – 'Bor-ing!"' he mouthed: *'Bor-ing!'* Still ruffled, he went back down on the shot – immediately miscued and threw the frame. Perkins looked out at the patio. The German couple were sitting on loungers about twenty yards away, in the shade. She was reading a book but he appeared to be taking a nap, so Perkins decided to leave him in peace – at least for a frame or two. He was on a roll now and wanted to take full advantage of it.

The band played on and the dancers continued to glide down Memory Lane…*We'll Meet Again, White Cliffs of Dover, Keep Your Sunny Side Up*…Frame followed frame and Perkins was up against it once more and rapidly beginning to lose interest and heart. Perhaps they should have gone swimming after all, or even souvenir-hunting with their wives.

His attention momentarily drifted back out to the patio. There was something going on out there. A group of people had gathered and were talking animatedly. Perkins took his next shot, with one eye on the patio and one on the pot. Two waiters had now lifted up a sun-lounger, with a man still sitting in it, and were carrying it towards the recreation area. It looked like the German…with his female companion and several other hotel staff and holidaymakers in tow. Someone opened both of the patio doors and the little party struggled in with the lounger and set it down beside the pool table. One of the Hotel managers came hurrying over with another waiter. Perkins put down his cue and quickly removed their drinks from the bench but Ray had his back to all this and was blissfully unaware of the unfolding drama. He gave a whoop as he made a pot but quickly stepped aside when Perkins nudged him and drew his attention to the little cortège that had stopped just feet away. The German was lifted from the lounger and laid full-length on the bench.

His companion removed his sunglasses but his eyes were closed and his face expressionless. Perkins and Ray edged further back behind the table. The woman held his hand and smoothed his head whilst simultaneously trying to converse, in monosyllables, with the Tunisians. Everyone moved urgently but in slow-motion, speaking in hushed tones. The Manager double-checked on the man's heart and felt again for a pulse. He called for a blanket and one was quickly brought and draped over the prostrate figure, leaving the head still uncovered. Nobody seemed certain what to do next. Eventually, a middle-aged man in Bermuda shorts came in from the pool, saw what was happening and strode up to the dance floor: 'Excuse me, ladies and gentlemen!' he called out, 'Is there a doctor in the house? We have an emergency situation here…' There was no response although, by now, some of the dancers must have been aware of what was going on. No-one switched off the music or toned it down or stopped the proceedings in any way. The man repeated his announcement. The music played on and round and round the dancers went, smiling fixedly at their partners, no-one wanting to believe – or so it seemed – the unthinkable, what with the sun shining outside, the music playing and the handsome, white-coated waiters everywhere to-ing and fro-ing with food and drink and bonhomie in abundance.

The man in the Bermuda shorts made one final appeal, though by now it seemed utterly redundant: was there a doctor in the house – anybody with first aid or medical experience? He waited for a response but they all went on dancing, as though they hadn't the remotest idea what was happening on the other side of the room – the other side of the universe – to one of their number.

When the music eventually cut out, they stood there, at a loss, waiting for it to start up again. The dead man – his tan already fading from him – was completely covered up and whisked away as discreetly and with as little fuss as possible, the woman silently weeping in his wake.

After they'd gone, the turntable began to spin again – this time with a slow, smoochy number. The two pool players looked at each other, stunned into silence. Ray held a hand across his chest as if to say *'Heart!'* Perkins nodded, noticing for the first time the dead man's coin still resting on the table where he had left it.

Second Coming

It must have been about halfway through *The Fugitive* – just at the moment when, lights flashing, sirens wailing, a fleet of police cars were skidding to a halt outside the seedy lodging house where Harrison Ford, alias Richard Kimble, was lying low – that the knock came at the front door. Perkins hit the remote, blanking the screen and, in one instinctive movement leapt from his armchair and dived under the kitchen table. His wife stayed on the settee and, only when the second knock came – a minute or so later – did Perkins realize she was asleep.

It was a late August evening but there was still some daylight left outside. From where he was crouched, Perkins was still not visible from the front window, but could easily be seen from the smaller, kitchen window, to his left. Another knock came at the door. He crawled over to the Welsh dresser, leaving himself briefly exposed in the gap between settee and wall and paused to take stock. Should he stay put or make a dash for the lounge? There was a small, free-standing mirror above him on the dresser. He took it down and slowly angled it out into the passageway so that he could see without being seen. Clearly visible through the frosted glass of both front and inner door, was the black – but unmistakable – blur of a figure. It's back was to him, as though its owner was looking out to sea. Perkins withdrew the mirror and turned to get up, intending to alert his wife but she was already crouching behind him. 'It's *Oswald,*' she said. 'I could see him through the blinds. Did you lock the front doors when you came in?'

'I think so.'

'You *think*!'

'I can't remember – I'm not sure. '

He extended the mirror back out into the passageway. The shadow moved away to the right and in a moment they could hear the rap of knuckles on the bay window.

'You'd better answer it this time,' she said. 'Bugger the film – we could be here all night!'

'No chance,' Perkins said. 'He's going to have to smoke us out first.'

'But he might walk in – '

'Stay here,' he said, 'and keep your head down. I'll try and lock the hallway door – ' Before she could argue, he made a sudden dash down the passageway, slid home the bolt of the hallway door, turned and bounded up the stairs three at a time, finally flattening himself against a wall of the landing.

The cat was on the top stair, gazing down at him as he lay there panting, her eyes registering indifference rather than surprise, as though nothing about Perkins or his eccentricities *ever* surprised her.

There was another rap on the front door. Perkins glanced down through the banisters then scrambled, at a crouch, into the front bedroom, although there was absolutely no possibility of him being spotted now, except by the cat. With the hallway door safely bolted and his wife more or less under cover, there was no more to be done – except wait. He flopped down on the bed and flicked on the portable television with the remote, mindful to lower the volume first. The screen flickered into life and he saw, with no surprise – since he had seen the film at least three times before – that it had all been a false alarum! The police hadn't come for Kimble after all – they'd come for the landlady's shady-looking son, whom they were now manhandling into the back of a car, leaving Kimble free to fight another day.

After a rap-less ten minutes, Perkins judged it safe enough to venture downstairs again but as he reached the landing the phone went. His wife came hurrying out of the kitchen – 'Don't answer it!' he said. 'Wait for the rings!'

They waited for the rings to end, the OGM to silently play and the caller's voice to kick in. There was a long, breathy pause before it did…*'Hello, Alvin,'* it said, in a familiarly remote sort of way – like a spaced-out speaking clock, *'are you there?…this is me, Oswald…I called just after eight this evening but, sadly, you were out…I wanted to make you an offer – an offer you couldn't refuse…but I can't discuss it over the* phone – for obvious reasons – except to say that it's a business proposition and there could be money in it…' the voice paused, as though to allow the word money to register to maximum effect '…hello, Alvin?…are you there?…obviously not…so I'll call back in a day or two to talk things over…and maybe we can start making plans…like I say: there could be money in it – not a lot but some – and you're just the man I need to come in on it with me…so, take care now – and remember: whatever you do, don't let the bastards grind you down…' There was a click and the line went dead. Perkins' wife quickly removed the phone from the hook. 'No, don't do that,' Perkins said. 'If he rings again, he'll know we're in – and then he'll be back!'

She replaced the receiver. 'What was all that about *'a business proposition?'* she said. 'And what did he mean by *'don't let the bastards grind you down?'*

'Christ knows!' Perkins said. 'I think he was speaking in tongues again.'

'He's not expecting you to put up any money, is he?'

'Well, he's come to the wrong place if he is,' Perkins said. 'I haven't got two pennies to rub together! Everyone knows that.'

His wife went back out the kitchen and Perkins followed. 'How did he get our number, anyway?' she asked.

'I gave it to him,' Perkins said.

'Oh, that's *great!*' she said, 'You actually *gave* him our number. Now he'll be ringing every five minutes.'

'I told him to ring before he came to the house again,' Perkins explained. 'At least, that way, I thought we'd be forewarned. Then we could always say we were on our way out.'

She lit the gas under a still-warm kettle and Perkins opened the microwave. The pizza he'd put in there just before Kimble leapt from the top of the dam, was already cold but he got two plates and started slicing it up anyway. 'I'm fed up with this,' she said. 'Every time we sit down for a quiet evening, Oswald turns up. I've had a hard day. I want to relax. It's just not fair – '

Perkins didn't think it was fair either but quickly reminded her that *she* was the one who'd invited Oswald to call at the house in the first place. She'd met him in the street several months before, by chance, took pity on him and told him to call in whenever he happened to be in the area. That was at least twenty visits ago.

'I only asked him in passing,' she said. 'Because he seemed lonely – and you hardly ever see anyone these days. I thought it would be company for you. After all, you taught with the guy for years – you had to have *something* in common.'

'We *do*,' Perkins said, 'we're both several sandwiches short of a picnic – but *he* hasn't even got a *hamper*. You should have asked me first. I could have warned you what would happen. He's a nice enough bloke – and gifted – but a lost soul. Show him a bit of human kindness and he attaches himself. Like a dog. And then you're stuck with him – for *life*. I told you before: he's on a different planet to the rest of us. That's why they had to give him the push in the end. Always sticking his neck out and putting his foot in it. Always saying exactly what he felt to whoever he liked. No discretion. No sense of self-preservation whatsoever. His heart's in the right place but he's got a huge personality disorder. Something to do with his endomorphs. The receptors in his brain just aren't getting the messages they should be getting. So he gets these uppers and downers. Van Gogh had the same problem. At the moment he's on an upper but he keeps leaving off his tablets and drinking and then he just goes haywire. Apparently, he painted himself red the other day – all over – and was prancing around naked in the street, claiming to be the Messiah. They had to take him in.'

His wife dropped two tea-bags into a teapot. 'What about those other friends of his?' she said. 'Don't they look after him?'

'He quarrelled with them,' Perkins said. 'That's part of his problem – they *care* about him but he's always quarrelling with them – usually over something trivial. They've *all* got personality disorders of one kind or another.'

'But why do they always seem to pick on you?' she said. 'It's almost as if they identify with you in some way. You're like a magnet for them!'

'Search me,' Perkins said. 'I wish I knew.'

'Well, I can't keep hiding behind the furniture every time he calls,' she said. 'I'm sixty-three. I've got bad legs – all this crouching isn't doing them a bit of good. He's your friend. Why don't you just go to the door when he calls and say it's not convenient. He'd understand. Or why don't you just tell him not to call again – *ever*?'

'I can't hurt the guy's feelings like that,' he said. 'Not all in one go anyway. He's harmless enough – he just needs somebody to talk to. I thought maybe if he kept getting no answer when he called then, sooner or later, he'd get the message.'

She got cups from the cupboard and milk from the fridge. 'It's better to be straight and up-front with the guy,' she said. 'What do you think he wanted this time, anyway?'

'Probably the same as he wanted last time *and* the time before,' Perkins said: 'company, a sympathetic ear. You know what he's like. He wants to talk about the finer things in life: Poetry and Art. To discuss some new hair-brained project of his for some multi-media conceptual piece of Art that's never ever going to see the light of day. He wants to involve me in some way but I've told him over and over that I've got enough projects of my own on the go already.'

His wife made the tea and poured it and they went back into the front room with their cups and two cold slices of pizza. 'It wouldn't be so bad if he was just in and out,' she said, 'but he stays for *hours* – talking about nothing. And his personal hygiene leaves a lot to be desired. Did you notice his feet? The smell nearly knocked me over.'

'*Please!*' Perkins said. '*not* while I'm eating!'

'Well, he's not our problem tonight, anyway,' she said. 'so maybe now we can put our feet up and watch television – ' She went over to the window to close the Venetian blinds but recoiled suddenly, as from a sudden blow: 'Oh my God – *he's still out there!*' she said. 'He's sitting in one of the deck chairs – '

Perkins jumped up from the settee, which he had only just flopped down on, nearly choking on a mouthful of pizza in the process: 'Doing what?'

'Looking at the view, I think – and drinking. He's got a bottle with him.'

Perkins joined her at the window. Just four feet away from them, they could see the top of Oswald's head above the back of the deck-chair. He had a bottle in one hand and a mobile held to his ear, in the other. Perkins and his wife backed away. The phone went.

'Don't answer it!' Perkins said. 'Let it ring.'

They waited for the rings to end and the OGM to finish playing… then a voice cut in – the same one they'd heard less than twenty minutes before, but more slurred now and with a slight edge to it: 'Hello Alvin,' it said, '…s'me again – Oswald…Don't tell me you're still not in! I'm sitting at the top of your steps – in your deck-chair…s'too nice to go back to the flat just yet so I got a bottle at the Off Licence and came back… 's a beautiful summer's night out here…you should see the view – magnificent!…you're a very lucky man to have all this on your doorstep, Alvin…and I'm a very lucky man to be sitting here looking at it: all those yachts out there, just starting to drift back in…sun going down over Oystermouth…blood-red like an orange…puts me in mind of Munch…very expressionistic – gives me an idea for a painting of my own: silhouetted figure at the top of the steps, pitch-black against a purple-red-orange backcloth of sky…moon and faint white sails in the distance…what d'you think? Possibilities, eh…? Poetry in paint! That's what I'm aiming for, Alvin. Just like you: poetry in paint! And you should see this sunset…s'like – Caspar David Freidrich…d'you know the painting I mean?…two men looking up at the moon…Tree of Life towering up in the middle…hey diddle diddle, the cat and the fiddle, the cow jumps over the… scuse me a moment while I get my little dictaphone out…I can feel some poetry coming on…Been doing a lot of this lately – instant poems! Hundreds of them – all dictated in situ, wherever I happen to be. Going to collect them all in a book some day soon…so here goes – ' There was a click and a faint whirring sound and then '…*Blue yachts – blow yachts on blissfully sun-blighted waves as the sky reddens and…reverberates…first star, startlingly white, stirring in my heart…sail souls – sail over sunken rocks*'…Alvin, did I tell you I've got a bottle of wine here? 'S a shame you're somewhere else. We could have got drunk together, watching the sun go down…and I had this business proposition I wanted to put to you. Well, more 'artistic' than 'business' - but doesn't look as though I'm going to be able to. Not tonight anyway. Pity. I need your help – your expertise. Thought we might try and write an opera together – not a crappy conventional opera: an experimental, holistic, multi-media one. About the sea. I've got a lottof ideas I want to share with you – tapes, sketchbooks, photographs…I want to include music, sculpture, photography, painting and poetry – maybe even drama n dance as well. We could include some of your poems and paintings – and mine... s'never been done before – not in the way I envisage it...and I'm almost certain I can get funding...' They could hear him take a prolonged gulp at the bottle...'Been hiding our talents away for too long, Alvin... locked out in the wilderness – all those philistines cold-shouldering us, trying to screw us up...but now's the time to play our hand – show those talent-less charlatans just what we can do...I really respect your work, Alvin – s'got honesty and integrity...you're one of the true poets of our time...so please ring me, if you can...let me know what you think...' There was a long pause. It was getting dark outside but when they edged forward they could still see him, sitting there in the gathering dusk, still with the mobile pressed close to his ear. They watched him take another long swig from the wine bottle – and then another: '...Where are you anyway, Alvin?' he said, 'Down the beach somewhere? On holiday?...Not for long, I hope...time's of the essence – don't want some swine stealing our thunder, do we? Gotto strike while the iron's hot... But is getting late now, Alvin, so I better get back – and maybe I'll see you in a day or two and we can start making plans. I'm really excited about all this...S'going to happen – I know it is. What was it Nietzsche said: 'You need Chaos t'give birth to a dancing star...'

    The voice cut out again and the line went dead. Perkins' and his wife melted further back into the room, in anticipation of Oswald getting up, but he remained seated. They waited and waited, the sky turning a deep purple, the sea imperceptibly shifting from puce to black. But, for a long time, Oswald stayed put. Then, as they looked, he took a miniature camera from his inside pocket and pointed it straight ahead at the sea. There was a flash. Then he pointed it at the Docks, two miles away to his left – another flash – and then at the lighthouse, five miles away to the west – a third flash. He panned around, seeming to search for something that had escaped his eye but, not finding anything, finally pointed the viewfinder up at the cloudless night sky. He took shot after shot then, of the same full-moon, each flash throwing his head into instant silhouette, starkly illuminating the plants and the flowers which surrounded him and the dark, shadow-filled room behind him, where Perkins and his wife clandestinely cowered.

Beauty and the Beast

Perkins had hitched up his newly-pressed chinos to just short of the knees, when the minor contretemps with his wife abruptly escalated into first shouts then screams as she started chasing him down the passageway with a carving knife. They'd done two circuits of passageway, kitchen and living room, before Perkins had finally tripped himself up on the chinos and collided with a small self-assembly coffee table – which they'd only recently bought from Ikea – completely demolishing it. It looked like the end of the start of a beautiful evening out. He'd picked himself up without delay and made an undignified exit, almost minus the chinos, reaching the bottom of the garden steps and his car before realizing that, in his haste, he'd picked up the wrong fleecy jacket. The one which contained his car keys and cash point card and at least ten pounds in cash, was still indoors and the one he'd snatched from the bannister on his way out – an almost identical one of his wife's – contained less than two pounds in small change and very little else. So he wouldn't be able to take the car, or sleep in it, or go anywhere far or buy anything much – couldn't even get back into the house, even if he'd wanted to. And his ribs, which had taken the full force of the fall, were killing him.

He'd walked around Town for a long time after that, looking in shop windows, wandering up back alleys, trying to get his head together, before he'd eventually found the haven of *Bangers 'R' Us* – an all-night café at the top of High Street. A Late Night Evening Echo from the railway station across the way, a round of toast, three cups of coffee and now this, his fourth and final cup, were just about all his finances had stretched to. He'd read the paper from cover to cover – including all the obituaries, the lonely-hearts columns and the small ads. As well as the money, he'd found a small, spiral ringed notebook in one of the coat pockets and that now lay open in front of him, ready to be written in, in the highly unlikely event of sudden literary inspiration.

The place was three-quarters full of late-night clubbers by the time Perkins was on his last coffee and several clues into the Echo's crossword puzzle. The fat man bounced in around two or three in the morning and sat down at an adjacent table, wedging himself into the gap between table and chair, his back to the window. He looked like Canon, the TV detective, only a spongier, more heavily upholstered version. When the waitress came to take his order, he ran his eye up and down the battered, ketchup-stained menu, like some kind of gourmet about to make a very shrewd and considered selection.

'What'll it be?' she said, wiping the table down for him with a damp cloth.

He slapped the menu shut, pushing it away from him with a satisfied grin: *'You* know what I want,' he said. 'I'll have what I *always* have – the *usual.*'

'What's that?' she said. 'Beans on toast? Toasted teacake…?'

'The Beast,' he said. 'Jus gimme **The Beast!.**'

The waitress went on wiping. *'The Beast?'* she said. 'Ooh, I don't know about that. D'you think you're up to it? Look at you – you got nowhere to put it.'

'I'll show you where I'll put it,' he said, rubbing his sides with two podgy white hands. 'Just bring it ere!'

She went away laughing and Perkins filled in another clue and tried not to stare.

The place was starting to get more interesting now. Besides the fat man, there were a man and a girl occupying the two tables behind him. He could see their shadows in the plate-glass window. For some time the man, who was in his early forties, had been trying to engage the girl in conversation, rabbiting on about anything and everything – trying hard to sound young and interesting. They were both a bit drunk and had begun to sing along to the jukebox.

The waitress reappeared bearing a plate the size of a dustbin lid, piled high with food: eggs, bacon, sausages, cockles and lava bread, fried bread, black pudding, potato fritters, tomatoes, mushrooms, baked beans, toast – and came and laid it down in front of the fat man. 'One **Beast!**' she said, and stood there, arms folded, as though defying him to eat it. The fat man picked up his knife and fork and sat looking at it for a moment or two, relishing the prospect. 'You'll *never* do it,' she said. 'Never in a million years!'

'Won't I?' he said, shaking the sauce bottle over the steaming mound, 'Jus watch me – !'

Through the wrought-iron bars of the window Perkins could see skyline above the Station roof, with no hint of dawn in it, as yet. His reflection stared back at him, dark-eyed and gaunt, pen poised over all the empty spaces. He had only a mouthful of coffee left in his cup and that had long gone cold. Before long, he gave up on the crossword and tried to write something in the notebook – something about the hours-old argument, its mystifying causes, something about the fat man sitting next to him and the couple behind him. After only a line or two, he turned to the back of the book. There was some writing there – about twenty pages of it, in his wife's hand: notes and jottings and doodles mostly, going back over several years, it seemed – some dated, most not. He started reading a random entry, which appeared to be an account of a meeting she'd had with her mother, some time before she died. In it, her mother had nagged her about the colour of her hair, which she'd dyed bright red, and her dress sense, which she thought let her down – cheapened her in some way. On another page was an account of one of his poetry readings – a reading which Perkins couldn't remember ever having given – in which he was afterwards surrounded by a bevy of beautiful and fawning, young women. On yet another page were what seemed to be descriptions of Native American and primitive tribal ceremonies involving eagles, wolves and buffalos. And on yet another was a scribbled telephone number, a date, and a single name in block capitals: FRANK OR-LOFF.

Perkins closed the book. The man behind him had now started a kind of musical game with the girl. He'd hum a classic theme tune to a movie or a TV programme and she'd have to supply the words. For some reason, most of his selections were from Westerns, which were either too old or too esoteric for her to get. Some she knew vaguely, but most she didn't – in which case the man would sing the words for her. Perkins, and the rest of the café, were being treated to a whole medley of tunes: *'High Noon'*… *'Maverick'*…*'The Man from Laramie'*… *'Streets of Laredo'*….The girl was impressed, not by his voice – which was really quite ordinary – but by his phenomenal memory, which stretched way back to the Fifties and beyond. 'Oh, you had me there,' she kept saying. 'That was way before my time. That was out of the *Ark*, that was.' Encouraged, he hummed one tune after another but before long she got bored and impatient for her turn. 'Come on – you gotto give me a chance now,' she said, ' – or I'm not playin.' She hummed the opening bars of *'My Way'* and the man pretended not to recognize it: 'Oh, that's a tough one,' he said. 'Pass!' She started singing it but was out of tune and got bogged down on the words half way through. Several of the other diners tried to help out and before long the entire café – including Perkins – were singing *'My Way'* at the top of their voices and totally out of sync. It was in the middle of this cacophony that Perkins' wife suddenly appeared. In the heat of the moment, he hadn't seen her come in but there she suddenly was, standing in front of him, hands on hips, wearing his black fleecy jacket, which was a couple of sizes too big for her. Perkins immediately stopped singing. She looked tired and gaunt as she flopped down in the seat opposite him. 'Well, what's happening?' she said.

Perkins didn't know what she meant. He picked up his pen and went on with his crossword puzzle, as though that was what he'd been doing all along. 'What d'you mean: *what's happening?*' he said.

She snatched the paper out from under his hand and folded it shut. 'I mean what's happening with *us*? Are you going to stay here all night singing old Sinatra numbers or are you coming home?'

Perkins sat back and capped his pen. 'I haven't decided what I'm going to do yet,' he said. 'I'm still trying to get my head straight. How did you know I was here, anyway?'

'A process of elimination,' she said. 'I knew you wouldn't be in your studio because you went out with my coat on and I found your keys. I knew you wouldn't get far without those. You weren't in the snooker hall and I knew you couldn't have gone drinking because everything's shut.'

'I might have left Town,' Perkins said.

'You didn't have enough money. You went without your Visa card as well – so you only had a couple of quid on you, at most. Where've you been all night?'

'My Way' had run out of steam by now and the diners were singing several songs simultaneously, one table competing against another. The fat man – his forehead beaded with sweat, his lips shiny with grease – seemed oblivious to everything bar his Beast.

'In here mostly,' Perkins said. 'I walked around for a bit, looking in shop windows, sitting on benches, reading the paper. Trying to keep warm – and, *oh, yes!*' he said, on a sudden inspiration, 'I did nip into Casualty about my ribs. They seem to think I may have broken one or two.'

'Don't expect any sympathy from me.' she said. 'You could have stayed and worked things out instead of running off like that. It was so bloody childish. Where else have you been? You weren't here when I looked in, two hours ago.'

'I was probably over the railway station then.'

'Doing what? Train-spotting – or waiting for the Chattanooga Choo-choo?'

'Buying a newspaper. Sitting down on a bench – thinking.'

'About what?'

'About us. Wondering why we can't seem to have a simple conversation these days without one or other of us flying off the handle. I was trying to decide whether it was time to call it a day, if you must know – whether it was time to finish.'

'To *finish*,' she said. 'What kind of language is that? That's the way teenagers talk: d'you want to *go* with me? D'you want to *finish* with me? Grown-up people don't talk like that. That's half your trouble: you've never grown up. You're still an adolescent – '

For the first time, the fat man actually glanced up from his food, looked at Perkins and his wife but then quickly went on eating. 'Well, what d'you want to do?' she said. 'I can't hang around here all night. I need to know where I stand – so I can plan my life. Just tell me what you've decided.'

'I haven't decided anything,' Perkins said. 'I need more space – more time to think.'

'D'you want to get a flat? D'you want to move out? Go and live with your father? Is that what you want?' She leant forward and stared him straight in the eyes: 'Or perhaps you'd rather go and live with – *Laura Llewellyn-Edwards.*'

Perkins looked confused: 'Laura who?' he said.

His wife slapped a battered little address book on the table. 'I found this in your pocket,' she said. 'It makes very interesting reading. A lot of names and addresses I've never heard of before. Including Laura Llewellyn-Edwards's.'

Laura Llewellyn-Edwards? Perkins had to think. The book was at least three years old and the name meant nothing to him. Then he suddenly remembered: 'She used to work for an Arts Association,' he said. 'In the Literature Department. I had to write to her once about a Grant. I've never set eyes on her in my life, if that's what you're thinking.'

His wife looked unconvinced. 'I thought you might have been going to meet her here.'

'At three in the morning in Bangers R Us?' Perkins said. 'Yeah, that would be so romantic – every girl's dream.'

His wife read him out several other women's names, for each of which he had a logical and simple explanation: a magazine editor, a reporter, a BBC producer…She still looked unconvinced. 'There's a poem in here, as well,' she said, 'a Love one, by the look of it – '

Perkins made a grab for the book, snatching it from her hands. 'I haven't finished that one, yet,' he said. 'And in any case, it's an old one I've been revamping. It's gotto be at least thirty years old. Seemed a pity to scrap it completely.'

'Why all the secrecy then?' she said. 'What've you got to hide? Who's it *to*?'

'To *you*, of course,' he said. 'In fact, I seem to remember showing it to you once. You thought it was good at the time. But if you'd rather I dedicated it to someone else – '

The waitress passed them with two plates of food, making her way to the next table. His wife seemed momentarily pacified by his explanation. 'Have you eaten yet,' she said.

He shook his head. 'I've got exactly 22p left,' he said. 'I was saving it for a medium-sized pepperoni or a small baguette in Tescos. I can't make up my mind – '

She picked up the menu as the waitress came back: 'You look half-starved,' she said, 'and I don't feel like cooking when I get back. What're you having?'

'Nothing,' he said, 'this coffee'll do me.'

His wife turned to the waitress: 'He'll have what that man's having,' she said, indicating the fat man, 'and I'll have a cup of tea.'

The waitress scribbled down the order – *'One Beast and one cup of tea'* – and returned to the kitchen.

'A *Beast*' his wife said after the waitress had gone. 'Quite appropriate in your case, don't you think?'

'Except that I'm broke – ' Perkins said.

'Don't worry – it's on me,' she said. 'You'll need to build yourself up if you're sleeping rough tonight. There's a frost forecast.'

'I don't want charity,' Perkins said. 'Just peace of mind.'

'Don't we all?' she said, snatching back the paper and, for the first time, noticing the notebook, which had been under it. She picked it up and opened it, not recognizing it as her own. 'Where did this come from?' she said.

'It was in your coat pocket,' Perkins said. 'I was going to do a bit of writing in it but somehow I wasn't in the mood.'

She flicked the book open and read the few lines he'd scribbled. 'What's all this about a fat man?' she said, loud enough for the fat man to glance up from his food. Then she flicked through to her own handwriting at the back of the book and her mood quickly changed: 'Have you been reading this?' she said, thrusting the book in front of him. 'Have you been reading my dreams again?'

Perkins gave her a bemused look: 'Dreams?' he said. ' What are you talking about?'

'These!' she said.

'I saw some writing at the back,' he said. 'I thought it was some sort of diary.'

193

'These are my own personal dreams,' she said. 'They're private. How would you like it if I started prying into yours?'

The fat man and several other diners had caught the tone of her voice now and were all poised on his response. Perkins shrugged and said nothing, refusing to be drawn any further, embarrassed by all the attention they were suddenly attracting.

'And don't give me the old silent routine,' she said. 'It won't wash any more. What have you read?'

'Okay,' Perkins said, in a near-whisper, 'I did just happen to see one or two things: something about your mother and something about eagles and buffalos. I wasn't sure what it was all about.'

'They were *dreams*,' she said. This is my *dream* book. Everything in it's a *dream* and they're all *personal*.'

'And that was my *personal* diary and address book!' Perkins snapped back at her. '*Real* events and *real* people – but half of them I've never even met, never even bothered to get in touch with. They're just *contacts*.' He leant forward over the table: 'But if we're going to play the interrogation game,' he hissed: 'who's *Frank Orloff* and what's he to you?'

His wife laughed, mockingly: 'You know very well who Frank Orloff is,' she said, 'I've told you often enough. He's a Healer and he lives in Tunbridge Wells. I've seen him about twice in three years. He's worked wonders on my back.'

'I *bet* he has,' Perkins said. 'I bet he's a real expert on your anatomy – '

'If you don't believe me, give him a ring,' she said. 'Make an appointment. It might do you some good: he's an expert on *Anger Management*!'

She stood up, abruptly, pre-empting any retort. 'Anyway – do whatever you like,' she said. 'I'm not going to take any more of this crap. You can stay here and Karaoke the night away for all I care, or you can come home with me – now. I've got the car outside. But, either way, I want my coat back – because I'm not hanging around any longer. I've got a life to live.' Perkins took off her coat and handed it over. She took off his, flung it down on the table, picked up her notebook and walked briskly out without another word. Perkins waited a minute or two, in case she had a change of heart, then went back to doing the crossword puzzle. The fat man paused to smile across at him, winking knowingly as if to say *'Women!'* then started mopping up his plate with a final piece of toast.

The place had all-at-once lost its ambience – seemed suddenly drained of colour and life. Across the way, the skyline above the Station façade had lightened to a deep Vick bottle blue as the first taxi of the morning pulled into the forecourt. Perkins was already having second thoughts about not going home when he had the chance but when he glanced back towards the kitchen: here came the waitress with his Beast. He sat up straight in anticipation, moving the newspaper out of the way to make a space for it. He was tired and hungry now and could absolutely murder a meal but when he felt in his jacket pockets, they were empty: no money, no card, no keys, no wallet – no anything.

The waitress plonked the plate down in front of him: 'One *Beast* and one tea to follow,' she said, standing there arms folded for a moment – just as for the fat man – waiting for Perkins' reaction to the enormity of what he was taking on. Perkins felt slightly sick but started picking away at it anyway. The waitress left him to it. Hopelessly wedged in his seat – his face bright crimson, his plate shiny and clean – the fat man smiled across at him, encouragingly. Perkins picked sullenly on, one eye on the kitchen, one on the door, trying to gauge his chances of making an impromptu exit: of doing his second and final 'runner' of the night.

Medicine

There was only half an hour left of the Old Year in Wales but five and a half hours of it left in New York. When his wife went out in the hallway to make a long distance phone call to their son, Perkins went out in the kitchen and hastily removed a bottle of gin from the bottom cupboard of the Welsh dresser. He unscrewed the top, took a quick slug from it, topped up the bottle with water from the tap and replaced it in the cupboard, just seconds before she returned.

'He's not there,' she said. 'I hope he's alright. We'll ring him later.' She sat down next to him on the settee but soon got up again. There was a gory, oft-repeated New Year's Eve Thriller on TV that he wanted to watch but she didn't. She clattered about in the kitchen for a while, then came back in with a set of tarot cards she'd bought herself for Christmas and, at a most climactic moment in the film, asked him to go in the front room with her for a reading. 'Must I?' he said. 'I want to watch this.'

She wouldn't take no for an answer. The film could wait. Didn't he want to see what the New Year had in store for him? For them all? It wouldn't take long and he'd be amazed at the result.

Reluctantly, he went into the front room and sat down at the table and she dealt him his cards. They were based on Native American teachings and all of them had animal pictures on them, together with printed interpretations. She spread the nine cards out for him in a row, face down. Six of them were fairly unimportant, she said, and three of them very important.

'Just do the important ones,' he said. 'I want to watch the film.'

She wasn't sure how accurate it would be with just three cards but she let him put six cards back in the pack. He turned over the first of the other three to reveal a brightly coloured mouse. 'Jesus!' he said, 'A *mouse*! That's terrible. I was hoping for a tiger or a mountain lion.'

'There're no tigers in North America,' she said, 'but anyway, a mouse isn't necessarily bad – even a contrary one.'

'A contrary one?'

'An upside down one,' she said. 'You drew it upside down.'

He groaned. 'I knew I wouldn't be much good at this,' he said. 'Is there anything worse than an upside down mouse? Is it dead?'

'Of course it's not dead,' she said, picking up the card. 'Listen to this: *"You have let yourself become slovenly and have developed a disdain for authority and order. Bring Mouse Medicine to your life's chaos and you will soon have everything under control. Stop chasing your tail. Turn away from life's trivialities. Little Mouse needs to see the Big Picture."'*

'The Big Picture's nearly finished,' he said. 'Can't I watch the end of it?'

'Just these other two,' she said. 'They're your own personal ones: the ones you'll carry into the New Year with you. Turn another card.'

He turned over his second card: an Upside Down Turkey. 'My God this is getting worse,' he said.

'"*Turkey,*"' she read, '"*The Gobbler card: otherwise known as the Give-Away Eagle. The philosophy of give away was practised by many tribes. Simply stated, it is the deep and abiding recognition of the sacrifices of both self and others. People in modern day society should study the noble turkey who sacrifices itself so that we may live. In Turkey's death we have our life. Honour Turkey.*"'

'Is that good?' Perkins said.

'Of course it is,' she said. 'Turkey medicine means you're basically a very unselfish person. You have transcended yourself. Turn another card'

He turned the last of the three: 'A buffalo!' he said. 'That's more like it!'

'"*Beware of pushing yourself too fast in the physical world,*"' she read, '"*at the cost of your eternal partner The Great Spirit.*"'

'I thought you were my eternal partner,' he said.

'"*Slow down and get back to basics,*"' she went on. '"*Reconnect with the source of life. Because of its desire to give the gifts that its body provided, and because of its willingness to be used on earth for the highest good before entering the hunting grounds of spirit, Buffalo did not readily run from hunters.*"'

Perkins had heard enough. 'Are all the animals in that book suicidal?' he said.

'What do you mean?'

'Are you telling me that the buffalo *wanted* to be slaughtered. In all the Westerns I've ever seen, they've been stampeding like hell.'

'I'm only telling you what it says here,' she said. 'This all derives from the ancient teachings of the shamans. You don't have to accept it if you don't want to.'

He took the cards from her and began to shuffle them. 'Let me try it on you,' he said.

'I've *been* done,' she said. 'I did it on myself. I drew the Butterfly, the Ant and the Deer. The Butterfly means I share the colours of my creation with the world but I'm about to undergo some form of transformation. The Ant is for patience: knowing that what is mine will eventually come to me and the Deer is for gentleness.'

Perkins slapped the cards down on the table: 'So, to sum up,' he said: 'You're basically gentle and patient and I'm slovenly and egotistical. Somehow, I knew I wasn't going to come out of this very well.'

'I drew one each for Owain and Kay earlier on,' she said. 'The Weasel and the Beaver: energy and ingenuity and a love of family and home. It was very reassuring. I'm not worried about them any more. I'm not worried about any of us. This next year's going to be *our* year.'

'You've been saying that every New Year's Eve for the past thirty years,' Perkins said.

'This year's different,' she said. 'It's all there in the cards.'

Back in the living room, the credits were already rolling on the New Year's Eve film. It was exactly ten minutes to midnight in Wales and ten to seven in New York. Perkins went back out in the hallway and lifted the phone off the hook. His wife came out of the front room just as he pressed the first digit: '*I* want to speak to him first,' she said.

'You spoke to him first last time,' he said.

'Yes, but you spoke to him for longer.'

'Perhaps we'd better time each other, then,' he said. 'How long shall we give ourselves?'

'As long as we like,' she said.

'Say ten minutes each,' he said. 'It'll be fairer that way. And cheaper.'

'I'm not worried about the money side of it,' she said. 'This is New Year's Eve, in case you've forgotten and he's been ill. I'm going to speak for as long as I like. It's more important for me to speak to him anyway. I'm his mother.'

'So what difference does that make?' Perkins said.

'So he tells me things he wouldn't tell you: like if he's in any sort of trouble. Like how he's been feeling. Like if the tablets are working. Like if he's any better.'

'He can tell me all those things as well,' Perkins said. 'Any time he likes.'

She held her hand out for the phone. 'Okay,' he said, handing it over: 'Unlimited time each and bugger the cost. Just so long as he doesn't hear us arguing this time. He gets upset about it.'

She began dialling the number and he went upstairs. He lay down on the bed and very slowly and carefully – like a bomb disposal expert – lifted the extension phone off the hook. The first voice he could hear was Owain's. It still sounded a bit shaky but a lot better than when he had last spoken to him. His wife began telling him the latest news but stopped suddenly in mid-sentence: 'Hang on a minute, Owain,' she said. 'I think your father's on the other line. I can hear him breathing – ' Perkins quickly muffled the mouthpiece with a hand. 'Alvin,' she said. 'Is that you on the other line? You know I can't stand it when you listen in. Put that phone down now. I can hear you *breathing*!' Perkins stopped breathing. 'Alvin, d'you hear me?' she persisted. Very gently, he replaced the receiver and went downstairs. She glared at him as he passed her in the hall. She was telling Owain about the tarot cards she had drawn and how their troubles were nearly all in the past and how the New Year was going to be better all round for everybody and that once he was better he and Kay could both come over for a break. It would do them the world of good. Perkins went into the kitchen and poured himself another slug of gin, once again topping up the bottle afterwards with water from the tap. There were bagpipes playing on the TV now and men in kilts cavorting. He listened as his wife told Owain not to stop taking the tablets until he was completely better: for *his* sake and Kay's and everyone else's. He was well on the way to recovery: she could tell from his voice. The New Year was definitely going to be *their* year. It was written in the cards...

Perkins checked the time. There were only seconds left to midnight. He went out in the hallway and unbolted the front door and as he did so, bells started to chime on the TV and down in the Town. Rockets were already going off in the Bay and ships' hooters were sounding from across the Docks. People were out on their lawns and in the streets, shouting across to each other. His wife got up off the stairs and stood in the front doorway. 'Listen to this, Owain,' she said, holding the phone out, 'Listen to the hooters and the rockets...'

'Can you hear them, Owain!' Perkins shouted, unable to contain himself. He tried to take the phone back off her but she wouldn't let go. Owain's voice, tiny and disorientated, crackled from halfway round the world. Perkins tightened his grip and yanked...

'...he's by here, Owain,' his wife said, 'trying to take the phone off me...*Yes*: he's had a couple of drinks already. He doesn't think I know he's been at my gin!'

'No, I **haven't,**' Perkins yelled. 'I'm sober as a judge. She won't let me **speak – !**'

Rockets were exploding everywhere. Bells rang out and sirens klaxoned and people yelled from neighbouring gardens. The pair of them stood locked in mortal combat in the doorway – *Patient Ant* and *Magnanimous Turkey* – struggling for possession of their son's voice, a world away from them in time and space, as the Old Year went hobbling out and the New one came clamouring in...

Medical

As they pulled up in the hospital car park, Perkins reminded his wife for the fourth or fifth time that morning to *'be herself'*. After all, she didn't have to act ill: she really *was* ill. Any fool could see that. But it might be advisable, he told her, not to mention the HRT treatment. If they thought it was an hormonal problem, they'd think it was something that could be cured. Then they'd send her for treatment somewhere and the next thing she knew, she'd be better.

'Isn't that the whole purpose?' she said.

'You know what I mean,' he said. 'We don't want them to think there's an easy way of making you better, otherwise, before you know it, they'll say you are – '

She cut him short. His logic bewildered her and she'd had enough of pep talks anyway. Any more and she'd cancel the appointment there and then.

They got out of the car and went in through a side entrance marked Out Patients. Ty Thomas Taig was a private concern built in the grounds of the old, Victorian hospital on the edge of Town. His wife had been sent there for an appointment by the Gold Stallion Insurance Company before they would make a first payment on her invalidity claim. Perkins was more nervous about the appointment than she was and had been for days.

His wife gave her name at Reception and they sat down in an empty Waiting Room. It was hot in there and windowless, with oppressive walls covered in pink and red roses. His wife picked up a medical journal and immediately began reading but Perkins couldn't keep still and was soon complaining about the heat: 'It's like an oven in here,' he said, getting up to examine the wallpaper, '– and you'd think they'd have chosen nice restful blues instead of reds and pinks – '

'Stop moaning,' she said, 'or I'm going.'

He sat down – hot, flushed and miserable – sullenly watching her read. Five minutes passed. Then another five. 'Who *is* this guy

Madoc, anyway?' he said, 'And what d'you know about him?'

'He's a very nice man.' she said. 'Very sympathetic – according to Dr Kojak.'

'Yes, but he's working for the Insurance Company,' Perkins said. 'He's bound to be biased.'

'He's totally independent,' she said. 'He doesn't work for them. He can say what he likes.'

'Don't trust him,' he said. 'These psychiatrists are all the same. They twist everything you say – '

'Don't worry,' she said. 'I know *exactly* what I'm going to say. I'm going to tell him *everything*.'

Perkins didn't like the way she said *everything*. They'd had their ups and downs in the past but *'everything'* seemed to hint at some sort of exposé. He was about to tell her not, on any account, to bring *him* into the conversation, when the consulting room door opened and an unseen figure beckoned her in…

She seemed to be in there a very long time. After a bit, Perkins moved to the seat nearest the Consulting Room door but couldn't make out a word. At one point, he thought he could hear her crying, but couldn't be sure. He picked up the medical journal his wife had been reading, opened it, read two paragraphs of an article about Mad Cow Disease and closed it again. On the wall opposite was a framed jigsaw puzzle of Anne Hathaway's cottage and beneath it, an old, free-standing Singer sewing machine with a bronze dinner gong on it and a basket of dried flowers. He got up and went and looked at the jigsaw puzzle, puzzling over why anybody would want to frame it and why it was accompanied by such a curious conjunction of objects. It occurred to him then that the whole place might well be bugged and that the dried flowers might possibly conceal a miniature mike – courtesy of Gold Stallion. He examined them closely, was about to part the paper-dry petals when the Consulting Room door abruptly opened and his wife emerged, red-eyed and pale: 'He wants to see you next,' she said.

Perkins had been caught totally off-guard but it was too late to protest. Before he knew it he was in the Consulting Room, the door closing shut behind him.

Madoc was a short, little man with a wizened smile and a frail handshake. He motioned Perkins to sit down and sat down opposite him at his desk. There was a pause as he cast around for an opening, smiling down at his hands, which were spread out before him on the desktop. 'I think you know what this is all about, Mr Perkins,' he said. 'I've been asked by the Gold Stallion Insurance Company to write a medical report on your wife. Now, I've had a long chat with her – about some of the things that have been troubling her – but to get the whole picture, as it were, I'd like to hear your side of things.' Madoc's hands locked fingers, grappling one against the other. 'What, for instance,' he went on, 'do you see as some of her main problems: over the last year or two, let's say – '

Perkins took a deep breath: 'Well,' he began, 'there've been quite a number, really. I'm sure she's told you most of the main ones but basically, I would say she's definitely not been' – he groped for the *mot juste* – '"her old self" for quite some time now.' Madoc nodded, waiting for him to elaborate. There were only so many ways of saying somebody was totally knackered and Perkins didn't want to exhaust them too quickly. 'She's been tired, listless and extremely depressed,' he went on, trying hard not to make it sound too much like the script for a Sanatogen commercial. 'Completely lacking in energy and drive – that old *"get-up-and-go"* – ' Madoc kept smiling enigmatically, his hands at rest now, steeple-shaped beneath his chin. Perkins kept talking, hearing himself mount symptom on symptom, cliché on cliché. It took him a while to hit his stride but after he'd cited the stresses and strains of teaching, the enormous upheavals in the Education System, low pay, low morale, mountains of paperwork and the lack of the 'personal touch' in the classroom, Madoc started to look impressed and had even begun taking notes. 'And, of course,' Perkins dictated, 'Redeployment didn't help: being forcibly transferred from one school to another, really hit her for six. Gave her a feeling of total inadequacy – '

'And how long has this been going on?' Madoc said, still writing, but faster now.

'I would say,' Perkins said, carefully choosing his words, working his way to a pension-clinching finale, 'that for the past four or five years, and for six days out of every seven, my wife has been suffering from some fairly major or minor symptom: ranging from bad back, headache and palpitations to high blood pressure, asthma and deep depression – '

Madoc's hand was racing over the paper now. 'And what about sleep?' he said, without looking up. 'How's she been sleeping?'

'Rather erratically,' Perkins said. 'She's been getting these terrible dreams.'

Madoc's eyes lit up. 'Oh really?' he said. 'Dreams are a particular interest of mine. What sort of dreams?'

'Well, there's this one in particular,' Perkins said, irrepressible now, 'about a huge tidal wave – a 'tsunami' I think they call them – that sweeps in out of the Bay and swamps the whole Town. All that's left is a bit of the Civic Centre clock tower sticking up out of the water. In the dream, she's warned me time and again that this tsunami is coming but I won't listen and then, when it does come, I race down to my father's house to try and rescue him. Before it hits, she's running up and down the streets knocking on doors trying to warn everyone. She gets that one a lot. She wakes up in a cold sweat – tossing and turning. Sometimes it's so bad I have to sleep in another room.'

'How does the dream end?' Madoc asked.

'I'm not sure,' Perkins said. 'She's never told me. I don't think she manages to save anybody – or herself. I think she wakes up before the end.'

'And this wave: does it completely engulf her?'

'I think so – but to begin with, she's running from it, trying to get away.'

'Is she on her own – or are there other people with her?'

'On her own, I think. All the other people are inside their houses. Is that significant?'

'It could have a bearing. We'll have to ask her – ' He scribbled a note, put the pen down, leaned back with folded arms and smiled. Perkins felt pleased with himself – had the feeling he'd done quite well: excelled himself, even. 'And your wife tells me you are a writer,' Madoc said, totally at ease now. 'What sort of things do you write?'

Perkins smiled modestly. This was more like it: he could coast from here. 'Poems and stories mostly,' he said. 'But I'm also working on a novel.'

'And I suppose your interests lie mainly with the modernist writers – '

'I suppose so,' Perkins said.

'I like the Welsh englyn writers, myself,' Madoc said. 'I go to all the Eisteddfodau and it never ceases to amaze me how quickly the bards can compose, given a set theme. *Siarad Cymreig?*'

'No, but my wife does,' Perkins said.

'Yes – to get back to your wife,' Madoc said, suddenly businesslike again. 'As I told you before, this report is something of a formality I'm obliged to carry out at the request of the Insurance Company. You've both given me plenty of information but is there anything you'd like to add before I start writing it up?'

Perkins thought for a moment, ran through a quick check-list in his head: 'No, that's about it,' he said.

Madoc reached across and shook Perkins' hand, thanking him for his co-operation. 'Oh, and one other thing,' he said, as Perkins stood up. 'Your wife's dream. Could you call her back in for just a minute. I'd like to ask her about that.'

Perkins opened the Consulting Room door and called to his wife. She came back in, dry-eyed now and slightly bemused. 'All finished, Mrs Perkins,' Madoc said, 'but there's just one more thing. Your husband tells me that you dream a lot? And that you have some dreams that repeat themselves from time to time.

'Well, yes,' she said, glancing suspiciously at Perkins.

'I was thinking of the dream about the tidal wave,' Madoc prompted.

'Tidal wave?' she said.

'You remember,' Perkins said. 'You told me you get it all the time. The dream about the tidal wave coming in and swamping all the rooftops of the Town – '

His wife gave him a blank look.

'You *must* remember that one,' Perkins said. 'You've told me about it lots of times. You even wrote it down once – '

'Did I?' she said.

'Yes, you *did!*' Perkins said, in desperation. 'You can't have forgotten.'

She shook her head. Madoc looked disappointed. 'Any other dreams you get?' he persisted. 'Any repetitive dreams of any kind?'

She racked her brains, anxious not to let him down. 'Yes,' she said. 'Sometimes I get a dream that the bedroom window is wide open and I fly out through it and over the Bay. It's a beautiful, clear, moonlit night and I'm flapping my arms like wings and soaring high over the Channel – '

Madoc didn't seem too impressed by that one. 'Anything else?' he said. 'Dreams can tell us a lot about a person's state of mind.'

'And I dream about my father sometimes,' she said. 'That he's still alive, or that he's alive but dying – ' Her eyes started to fill up as she spoke. Madoc seemed about to question her further but stopped himself, sensing perhaps, that enough was enough. He stood up and thanked them both again, wishing them well and assuring Perkins' wife that the report would be completely impartial.

'Should be a piece of cake,' Perkins said, as they crossed to their car. 'I laid it on thick. Made everything sound ten times worse. We got on like a house on fire – '

'Yes, but what did he say about *me*?' she said.

'Not a lot,' Perkins said. 'We talked about literature most of the time: Welsh poetic metrics and the englyn. It was fascinating – '

'So, *I'm* at the end of my tether and you spend the whole time talking about bloody poetry. I might have guessed!' she said.

'You *were* mentioned,' Perkins said. 'Once or twice.'

'Be serious,' she said. 'You were in there an awful long time.'

Perkins laughed and wrapped an arm around her: 'Of *course* we talked about you,' he said, ' – a lot.'

'What did you tell him about me?' she said.

'Probably much the same as you told him,' Perkins said. 'That for the last four or five years you haven't been yourself. What did you tell him about me?'

'There you go again,' she said. '*Me! Me! Me! I'm* the one who's ill. He said I should take more care of myself, stop worrying about other people and enjoy life. He said we should go on holiday.'

'We will,' Perkins said. 'All in good time – '

'He said soon.'

'It will be.'

The doors to Out Patients swung shut behind them. 'And another thing,' she said as they crossed to the car park. 'Who told you you could discuss my dreams with a complete stranger?'

'He asked me about them.'

'Yes, but why did you tell him anything?'

'Because I wasn't expecting him to call you back in,' Perkins admitted. 'Because I thought he'd be able to tell something from them. And you've got to admit that wave one's very unusual. He'd probably be writing that one up for some medical journal at this very moment if you hadn't denied all knowledge of it. Why the hell did you do that? I felt a complete idiot. You nearly blew everything.'

'Of course I remembered it,' she said, 'but I've told you before: my dreams are *my* business. I don't want *everybody* knowing about them.'

They got in the car and Perkins switched on the ignition. 'He was really interested in how that dream ended,' he said. 'How *does* it end, anyway? Do I save my father? Do I save myself?'

'You both drown,' she said. ' – sunk without trace.'

Perkins eased his foot down on the accelerator and pulled out into the busy rush-hour traffic. 'And what about you?'

'and I live happily ever after,' she said, ' – *of course.*'

Apocalypse Then

1

That morning, Perkins was already dressed and ready to leave for his studio well before his wife woke up. He brought her up the mail and a cup of tea and sat on the edge of the bed with her, watching the end of the News on the portable TV. When it was finished, he got up to go but she stopped him, abruptly: 'No, don't go yet,' she said. 'Sit down. I've got something important to tell you.'

He sat back down, for some reason expecting the worst: shopping to be fetched, repairs to be done, bills to be paid. He didn't really want to know – not now he was on his way out, his day already planned. She seemed to read his thoughts: 'Although, maybe I shouldn't tell you,' she said. 'Maybe it's the wrong time.'

'Tell me,' he said. 'You've got this far.'

'You'll only worry,' she said.

'No, I won't,' he said, suddenly worried.

'Are you sure you want to hear it?'

'Either tell me,' he said, 'or I'm going. I've got a lot of work to do today.'

She turned off the TV and he knew it was important, then: anything less and she'd have just turned down the volume. She took hold of his hand and held it for a moment, with a terribly forlorn look in her eyes so that, suddenly, he saw way past the house and the mortgage and the red-lettered final demands, to growths and tumours and floral tributes round a deep black hole in the ground.

'I don't want anybody else to know about this,' she said. 'Not yet, anyway. They'll know soon enough. D'you promise?'

He promised.

'Some people know already – and some people just don't *want* to know.'

'What!' he said. 'For Christsake: **What!**'

She took a deep breath. When she let it out, he was totally unprepared: 'There's a cloud of photons heading directly towards the earth,' she said, 'and they reckon they're going to reach us before the millennium.'

Perkins breathed a huge sigh of relief: 'Thank God for that!' he said. 'I thought it was going to be something terrible. What's a proton?'

'*Photons,*' she said. 'I'm not exactly sure. But they're headed this way. Geena told me. She's seen a picture of them. It's like a big, huge wheel in space. An immense electro-magnetic force.'

'So, what if they *are* headed this way?' he said.

She shook her head, as though she was talking to a child: 'So some people are already preparing for it, now,' she said. 'Not many. Just a few, all over the world. Geena's one of them and now *we* need to prepare, too. All of us: you, me, Mathew, Èmilie, Owain, Kay, your father, my mother – '

'Why?' he said.

She looked at him again, as though she couldn't believe he could be so obtuse: 'Because when it passes the earth, there's going to be a great change. Nothing will ever be the same again. Eveything will be different.'

'How d'you mean?' he said. 'Like the end of the world or something?'

'Not the end of the world,' she said. 'But a lot of people are going to die and we need to be prepared, to protect ourselves.'

'Die of what?' he said.

'Of shock mostly,' she said, 'but other things as well: floods, earthquakes.'

Perkins was worried again. This wasn't like her. He'd never heard her talk this way before.

'The point is,' she said, 'when the photons pass the earth, everything's going to come to a stop. They'll interfere with our power sources. There'll be no electricity. No heat. No transport. No nothing. Everything'll be in total darkness. For two years.'

Two *years*! He'd been expecting her to say maybe an hour or two or a couple of days at most: 'Two *years*!' he said. 'That's a long time. Has there been anything in the papers about all of this?'

'I've just told you,' she said. 'Only a few people know about it and only a handful of those are taking it seriously. I'm telling you to give you a chance to prepare for it. To meditate. You need to open up your chakras in readiness.'

She'd expressed concern about his chakras before. He wasn't a total sceptic but, on the other hand, he'd never been totally convinced that he *had* any. 'How d'you know my chakras aren't open already,' he said.

'Because you haven't been on any courses,' she said. 'You haven't studied it all like I have.'

'That's a bit elitist, isn't it?' he said. 'A bit *holier than thou*? It's like saying: "You're thick because you haven't been to University." A lot of my chakras *are* open already, as it happens. I've been working on them a lot, in my spare time.'

'Well, I'm pleased to hear it,' she said, 'because the sooner they're *all* open, the better. There isn't much time. Some people in Australia have started already. And we need to prepare, too. Stock up for it. That's why I didn't want the chimneys blocked up. We're going to need those coal fires. And we need to get plenty of wood in. More oil lamps, candles, tinned food, that sort of thing. I want Owain and Kay to come back from America and Matthew and Èmilie to come back from London, to live with us, so we'll all be together. And you'd better give me your phone number down in the studio, in case it happens and I need to warn you. You're on the flat down there. Once the ice caps melt, it's going to be a bit like Noah and the Flood. If you're up on high ground you'll be alright. Millions are going to die – mainly from shock and floods and lack of provisions – but we'll be all right because I've been going on these courses and learning.'

Perkins still couldn't take it all in. Why hadn't he seen or heard a word about all this before? Was she sure there'd been nothing in the papers or on TV? Something like this should have been headlines.

'Maybe they don't want to panic people,' she said. 'Or more likely, they don't believe it *could* happen. There's some people – rich people – have already started building shelters to protect themselves. It's been predicted for a long time that this was going to happen. It's been prophesied. The Mayans knew about it and the Egyptians. Geena knows. She's seen a diagram – '

This wasn't looking good. Perkins was really worried now. And all the time she was telling him, she didn't seem worried about herself, more about him and what would become of him. He tried to laugh it all off – to put it in some sort of perspective – but she was in earnest. 'Well, if everything's going to be changed,' he said, 'Does that mean for the better or worse?'

'For the better,' she said, without hesitation.

'But if it's for the better,' he said. 'How come only the rich'll survive?'

'They won't,' she said. 'Even with their shelters. Only the ones who have prepared mentally *and* spiritually will survive. But we may eventually need to move from here. It's too near the sea.'

Perkins had no intention of going anywhere. '*You* move if you like,' he said, 'but *I'm* staying put. I'm happy *here*. I'll take my chances where I am. Just drop me a line now and again, that's all.'

'How can I drop you a line?' she said, 'If you're under fifteen foot of water!'

'You see,' she said, trying to put it as simply as she could, 'we *hav*e to change. Mankind can't go on living like this. Haven't you noticed how everything's been going wrong with the world lately?'

'Everything's been going wrong with the world for years and years,' Perkins assured her. 'For aeons – since the beginning of time.'

'But especially now,' she said. 'Particularly over the last couple of years. Think of Iraq and Yugoslavia and Northern Ireland. Think of the environment: the rain forests, the ozone layer, carbon emissions, nuclear fallout. Everything's gone corrupt and rotten. But all that's got to change. There's got to be a rebirth – a cleansing, a new world order!'

She was still holding his hand, squeezing it, willing him to understand. He didn't know what to say, what to tell her to prove it was all a load of old codswallop. That everything was going to stay the same – at least for their lifetimes. He was touched that she wanted him to survive but concerned that, for some reason, she seemed to think that *she* would survive and *he* wouldn't. He looked at his watch.

She let go of his hand, perplexed that he was in such a hurry to be gone: 'Go on then – *go*,' she said, 'if painting's more important. But the quicker you come to terms with all this the better. It *is* going to happen, there's no doubt about that. It's just a question of when...'

2

By evening, her mood had changed. It was as though the photons had never existed. They made tea and chatted about their day and all the normal, run-of-the-mill, non-life-threatening things they always talked about. Perkins produced a couple of holiday brochures he'd picked up in Town and they sat for a while flicking through them, trying to decide – with no sense of urgency whatsoever – where and when they'd like to take a much-needed break.

Afterwards, he went up to his room to do some writing and, while he was at it, happened to look up *'photon'* in the dictionary: *'a quantum of electromagnetic radiation,'* it said, *'regarded as a particle with zero rest mass and charge, unit spin and energy equal to the product of the frequency of the radiation and the Planck constant.'* He looked up *'Planck constant'*: *'a fundamental constant equal to the energy of any quantum of radiation divided by it's frequency,'* it said, *'with a value of 6.6262×10^{-34} joule seconds.'* None the wiser, he was about to check out *'Planck's law'* as well, when his wife called up to him.

He hurried downstairs with the dictionary, intending to baffle her with science, but he didn't get the chance. She was sitting in the quiet room with an atlas on her lap, open to a map of Wales, above which she was dangling her crystal pendulum. She had a look of intense concentration on her face and the crystal was ever-so-slightly vibrating. He watched her for a second or two, until: **'Twll!'** she said, stabbing at the map with a finger. 'That's *it!* Four hundred and seventy one feet above sea level and well inland. That's where the crystal says we've got to go...'

3

And so there they were three days later: standing in the car park of a remote, one-horse mountain village in mid-Wales on a bleak Saturday morning in February, lost and bewildered, like aliens beamed down from outer space. Neither of them had ever been to Twll before but that was where the crystal had directed them and who was Perkins to argue with the crystal? His wife was sure there'd be something there – a sign or a message of some sort – which would set them on the right track.

There was sleet in the air and a biting north wind. But why *here*? Perkins kept asking himself. 'Why *Twll*?' There must have been plenty of other equally suitable but far more attractive places to land up in – and who was to say that a draught hadn't come down the chimney at the precise moment the crystal was hovering over Twll and vibrated it – just enough to make it seem like a sign?

It took them some time to decide in which direction to head. There was a Tourist Centre right on the edge of the car park, so they opted for that…It was closed. They tried the Souvenir shop next door…That was closed, too. And so, it transpired, was nearly everything else within sight. Why, if the crystal knew so much, hadn't it warned them beforehand that nothing was ever likely to be open in Twll?

They walked past a rugby pitch and turned left into what turned out to be the High Street: the main artery and nerve centre of Twll…It was almost deserted. His wife hurried on like a woman possessed, searching for something, but not knowing what. As he watched her, the thought occurred to him that perhaps – God forbid – she *liked* it there already, but he couldn't see himself spending the whole of the Apocalypse in Twll. It would be a fate worse than death.

At last he spotted a couple of pedestrians – and a cat. A car passed right down the street but didn't stop. She was a long way ahead of him by now. He stopped to look in a tea-shop window. He didn't need to look at the chalked-up menu to know that everything was probably off, but there was a large sign next to it which caught his eye: **WHAT'S ON IN TWLL** it said in big, bold letters. And there, underneath – a whole month's calendar of days had been handwritten out with a Jumbo-sized felt tip pen: from February 1st to February 28th. But only two events had been filled in: a coffee morning at the local Junior School and a Gymanfa Ganu in the Chapel. All the other dates were blank.

When he looked round there was no sign of his wife. He hurried on in the direction she'd taken, anxious not to be left alone in that place, but she was nowhere to be seen. At the end of the High Street, just around a bend, was a church and he headed towards that. They'd already stopped at two chapels on the way up: two very remote places, with only a couple of dozen people buried in each. The oldest incumbent they'd come across was 92 and the youngest just six weeks, which made Perkins think that if the Apocalypse were to come there and then, at 53 and 55 respectively, they couldn't really grumble.

The graveyard of this church – St. Twll's or whatever it was called – had plenty of spare space left in it and, if the worst came to the worst and they had to move there, they wouldn't have any problem finding a plot. He walked down one path and up another musing that on a normal Saturday morning at that precise time, he'd have been walking up and down the aisles of Tescos, pushing a loaded trolley...

There was still no sign of his wife. It started to sleet, suddenly and without warning. He sheltered under an old yew tree with a semicircle of memorial plaques and a withered wreath for company until, gradually, it eased off. The sun came out. The paths were streaming wet and the gravestones glistening. He did a complete circuit of the churchyard looking for her and then, as he was about to give up and as a last resort, he tried the handle to the church. He might have guessed it would be one of the few places open in Twll. He went in, trailing his footprints across the echoing porch, and opened an inner door. It was even quieter in the main body of the church – a cold and melancholy, candlewaxy quietness. His feet made no sound on the carpet. There was light shafting down from a side window and there was his wife, standing half way down the aisle with her back to him, looking up at the altar. She hadn't heard him come in, or perhaps she had but she didn't turn round or acknowledge his presence in any way. He watched her for a moment. She was standing perfectly still, just beyond the shaft of light, in total communion with some *thing* or some *body*. And he wondered how long she'd been there, standing like that and what she was doing: whose damned or immortal soul she was praying for and if she'd asked, or was asking, if this was the place – really *The Place* – that they were meant to come to. He didn't want to disturb her just yet, so he retreated to the back of the church. There was a Visitors Book on a table and he signed their names in it: hopefully their first and last connection with Twll. When he thought she was ready, he walked back down towards her. She heard him coming and turned. She looked worn out. He put his arm around her. 'What's the matter with me?' she said, almost immediately. 'My mind is all confused. Am I going nuts or what?'

'Of course, you're not,' he said with a reassuring laugh. 'You're as sane as a church mouse!'

But she wasn't convinced. 'I don't know why we were supposed to come here,' she said. 'It's high up and it's far away from the sea but that's just about all it's got going for it. Maybe it's a question of us *having* to live here, eventually. When the time comes, we'll have no option. Do you think Noah wanted to live in an ark?'

Perkins didn't have an answer for that. At that precise moment, what he most wanted to say was 'For Christ's sake, let's get away from here – *fast*. I don't want to be seen dead or alive in Twll, let alone face the Apocalypse here…'

They walked back up the aisle, he with his arm still around her and when he spoke what he actually said was: 'Let's go home, love

– the cat'll have given up on us by now. Then we can have a Chinese in Town and go to the pictures or just get a take-away and a video and put our feet up by the fire...'

Also available from Moonstone:

Dreaming from North to South: New and Selected Poems by Alan Perry

'Alan Perry…is a gifted and humane man who is an underrated Welsh treasure. These poems bristle with the grit and substance of everyday life. They are immensely readable…a book that resonates with the joys and despairs of daily living. There is much humour in Perry's work and, always, understanding.'
Herbert Williams in Roundyhouse.

'There is a strong sense of place in the writing…and often a touch of poignancy. There is also humour and, in a time in which we hear complaints about the inaccessibility of much modern poetry, a lot of plain speaking. The pieces are lucid and immediate, unafraid to be domestic and yet nonetheless always mindful of the universal… there are many gems here that make this not only a successful collection, but also one that recognises the conflicts of writing poetry.'
Coffee House Poetry: Cinnamon Press.

'Accessible and enjoyable poetry. Alan Perry paints perceptive portraits of life…simplicity interwoven with a deeper complexity and thoughtfulness.'
The Big Issue.

'Winner of the Eric Gregory Award for poetry and the Leslie Moore Award for painting, he has in the past summoned up the dark, chaotic visual fantasy worlds that accompany a collection of children's poems by Vernon Watkins and exhibited paintings worldwide… Perry's poetry is full of the humour and poignancy of mundane, every-day encounters.'

Kate Lay in the South Wales Evening Post.

'An impressive collection that really shows the full range of this poet/painter's powerful writing skills. He has selected perfectly from CHARACTERS (1969) to WINTER BATHING (1980). The section NEW POEMS (2000-2005) is a welcome bonus for his many admirers.'

Peter Thabit Jones in The Seventh Quarry.

'...his style and subjects have always been 'natural and down to earth...There is a fine, tender succession of poems to and about Jean, his artist wife...The earliest group concern workmates on building sites and includes the well-known 'The Mimic', a good example of Perry's light, humorous touch...Perry's experience and development as a painter and art teacher inspire a number of poems...although his mother also taught art, more of his poems are concerned with his father whose practical trade, as an electrician, Alan did not follow but which his father keeps trying to pass on. It is this stubborn, ageing, garrulous figure which dominates the collection and to whom it is partly a memorial. However, the last poem (which gives the book its title) is a hopeful love poem looking to 'New Directions' in the future.'

Caroline Clark.
A review from www.gwales.com, with the permission of the Welsh Books Council.

'...Perry has never been one to kow-tow to the Establishment.'

Mike Jenkins in Red Poets.

'...one of the great excluded.'

Peter Finch in Planet.

U Turns: The Early 'Perkins' Stories by Alan Perry

'...picks out the absurd from the everyday to give an overall impression of Swansea, which contrasts the banality of small town life with an ultimate humour and affection for the City and its characters.'

Richard Jones in the South Wales Evening Post.

'captures perfectly the bleakness of a wet summer in a South Wales seaside resort and, by contrast, the warm, intimate life that continues in even the emptiest places on the inside, behind the curtains. Inside the skull. In the womb. Under the tarpaulin with the workmen...The dialogue is pointless, funny and authentic. You can hear the accent in the words. The vitality of the stories seems to lie in the atmosphere: terrible bleakness within which is the vivid consciousness of the main character. Peeling off the next layer you get to the private anxieties, then last to a springing hope.'

Gillian Clarke.

'These are fine stories...'
Angela Carter.

'**Books may be ordered online from either** *moonstone.press@ntlworld.com* or *www.gwales.com*